MEATLESS MEALS
FOR MEAT EATERS

MEATLESS MEALS FOR MEAT EATERS

OVER 150 DELICIOUS VEGETARIAN RECIPES

Miriam Barton

SILVERLEAF
PRESS

Silverleaf Press Books are available exclusively
through Independent Publishers Group.

For details, write or telephone:
Independent Publishers Group
814 North Franklin St.
Chicago, IL 60610
(312) 337-0747

Silverleaf Press
4110 South Highland Drive, Suite 340
Salt Lake City, Utah 84124

ISBN-13: 978-1934393468

TABLE OF CONTENTS

ACKNOWLEDGEMENTS

I would like to thank my husband for his supportive encouragement in the writing of this book, and my children for being willing taste testers. A special thanks goes to the several people who have known that I started working on this book and sent me positive energy, including Rick and Louise Swain, my sister Paula, and my taste-testing neighbors. I owe a big thanks to Kristin Wynder for helping get my website started, and for her computer know-how. Thanks go out to the team at Silverleaf Press, especially my editor Linda Mulleneaux for her positive encouragement and for giving me a chance in the first place. Thank you!

❧INTRODUCTION❧

This book is written for anyone who wants to live a healthy lifestyle. In the United States, we seem to have adapted an "it's not a meal unless there's meat" attitude. This probably stems from concerns regarding protein, iron, energy, or just wanting to feel satisfied after a meal. Actually, there are plenty of meatless sources of protein and iron. Meatless meals can be very substantial, and once you go meatless for most or all of your meals, you may find you have more energy than ever before.

Many medical studies have shown that a diet high in meat can lead to heart disease and cancer, the two leading causes of death in the United States.[1] The human body can take up to five days to fully digest meat, and because of the lengthy process, decomposition or a rotting process occurs, which causes dangerous bacteria to grow and, over a long period of time, can cause disease to set in.[2]

As far as the short-term effects of a diet high in meat, research shows that it strains the kidneys and liver, often induces allergies, and may deplete the body's calcium level.[3] The latter occurs because the acids necessary for the digestion of meat can only be absorbed in the presence of calcium. Therefore, if a person is calcium deficient, the mineral will be taken from the bones, thus contributing to bone loss and osteoporosis.[4]

The average American eats about one and a half times the daily recommended amount of protein.[5] Yet many people are concerned that if they eat less meat or no meat, they won't get enough protein. So how much protein does a human body really need? According to the USDA, the recommended daily allowance (RDA) of protein is 46 grams for women and 56 grams for men, though these figures don't take into account a person's body mass and level of physical activity. For pregnant or lactating women, 71 grams of protein a day is recommended. For children ages 1 to 13, the recommended daily intake of protein is 9 to 34 grams, depending on age. Keep in mind that there are countless plant-based as well as dairy and egg sources of protein.

For beginners, trying a vegetarian cookbook can be intimidating and discouraging, since many of the dishes taste foreign to people who are accustomed to meat-based meals. The recipes in this book are designed for a meat eater's palate. In other words, even a meat eater will find every recipe in this book tasty, satisfying, and even filling.

Many people say they would eat less meat if they knew how to make nourishing, delicious meals without it. If you are one of those people, look through this book and find the flavors and textures your family is accustomed to. Begin slowly, making one or two meatless meals a week, and gradually use this book more often until you and your family enjoy eating much less meat. You will find there is a world of flavor and health, and even healing, in the fruits, vegetables, grains, and legumes that nature has provided.

I hope *Meatless Meals for Meat Eaters* proves to be a treasured resource in your journey to a more healthy and energetic lifestyle.

Notes

1. See National Cancer Institute fact sheet, "Chemicals in Meat Cooked at High Temperatures and Cancer Risk," accessed Aug. 25, 2011, http://www.cancer.gov/cancertopics/factsheet/Risk/cooked-meats; Committee on Diet, Nutrition, and Cancer, Assembly of Life Sciences, National Research Council, "Diet, Nutrition, and Cancer," The National Academies Press, 106–116, accessed Aug. 25, 2011, http://www.nap.edu/openbook.php?record_id=371&page=R6; Sinha et al, "Meat Intake and Mortality: A Prospective Study of Over Half a Million People," *Archives in Internal Medicine,* 2009, accessed Aug. 25, 2011, http://archinte.ama-assn.org/cgi/content/full/169/6/562?maxtoshow=&hits=10&RESULTFORMAT=&fulltext=eating+meat+causes+heart+disease&searchid=1&FIRSTINDEX=0&resourcetype=HWCIT>.

2. See John McDougall, M.D., "Meat in the Human Diet," *The McDougall Newsletter,* accessed Aug. 26, 2011, http://www.nealhendrickson.com/mcdougall/030700pumeatinthehumandiet.htm; Milton R. Mills, M.D., "The Comparative Anatomy of Eating," accessed Aug. 26, 2011, http://www.scribd.com/doc/94656/The-Comparative-Anatomy-of-Eating.

3. Neal D. Barnard, "Health Risks of High-Protein Diets," *Good Medicine,* Autumn 2002, vol. 11, 3:12.

4. D.E. Sellmeyer et al, "A High Ratio of Dietary Animal to Vegetable Protein Increases the Rate of Bone Loss and the Risk of Fracture in Postmenopausal Women," *American Journal of Clinical Nutrition,* 2001, vol. 73, 1:118–22.

5. "Making and Maintaining Muscle: How Much Protein Do You Need?" National Institutes of Health, accessed Aug. 26, 2011, http://newsinhealth.nih.gov/2008/March/docs/01features_01.htm; Miriam Nelson, M.D., "Will Eating More Protein Help Your Body Gain Muscle Faster?" reviewed by Gary Vogin, M.D., accessed Aug. 26, 2011, http://www.medicinenet.com/script/main/art.asp?articlekey=50900.

DAIRY AND EGG DISHES

BUTTERMILK HONEY PANCAKES

These pancakes melt in your mouth! Top them with 100% maple syrup.

1 large egg
1 cup flour
1 cup buttermilk
2 tablespoons honey
1 tablespoon canola oil
1 teaspoon baking powder
½ teaspoon baking soda
¼ teaspoon salt
butter
chopped pecans (optional)

1. In a medium mixing bowl, beat the egg until fluffy. Add remaining ingredients and mix thoroughly.
2. Heat griddle or large frying pan over medium heat, then lightly coat with butter. For each pancake, pour about ¼ cup batter onto heated griddle or pan. Flip pancakes when the batter looks bubbly on top. Cook for another minute or until golden brown on each side.

Makes 4 servings.

Nutrition Tip: Pecans are high in protein, iron, folate, vitamin A, fiber, calcium, and potassium, as well as omega-3 and omega-6 fatty acids.

❧ BANANA BERRY FRENCH TOAST ❧

This is a scrumptious way to eat breakfast, as well as a great way to get more fruit in your diet. The French toast is delicious with or without the Banana-Berry Topping.

12 slices soft bread
4 eggs
¼ cup milk
1 teaspoon vanilla
2 dashes cinnamon
butter
Banana-Berry Topping (see below)

1. Make the Banana-Berry Topping.
2. Heat griddle or frying pan to medium heat and lightly coat with butter.
3. Beat together eggs, milk, vanilla, and cinnamon until smooth. Dip both sides of each slice of bread in the egg mixture.
4. Cook bread until eggs are done, about 2 minutes each side. Top with Banana-Berry Topping.

Makes 4 servings.

❧ BANANA BERRY TOPPING ❧

This topping is delicious on French toast, as well as crepes, pancakes, waffles, and yogurt.

1 banana, peeled and sliced
1 cup sliced strawberries
1 cup blueberries, raspberries, or blackberries, or a mixture of all three
2 tablespoons honey

Combine berries with banana and honey. The longer the berries sit in the honey, the sweeter and juicier they will be.

PUMPKIN FRENCH TOAST

This breakfast meal will win over any holiday guest.

10 slices bread
½ cup cooked, puréed pumpkin
3 eggs
¼ cup milk
1 tablespoon agave nectar
1 teaspoon vanilla
¼ teaspoon sea salt
¼ teaspoon cinnamon
⅛ teaspoon nutmeg
⅛ teaspoon ground ginger
⅛ teaspoon ground cloves

1. Heat a large pan over medium heat, or a griddle to 300°F. Lightly coat the heated cooking surface with butter just before you start cooking the French toast.
2. In a large mixing bowl, beat all ingredients (except the bread) together until the egg yolks are smoothly incorporated into the batter.
3. Gently dip both sides of each piece of bread in the egg mixture just before placing on the griddle or pan. Cook the toast until the eggs are set, about 3 to 4 minutes on each side.

Makes 4 to 5 servings.

Nutrition Tip: Because of cinnamon's anti-inflammatory qualities, regularly eating the spice can reduce joint pain. Cinnamon also helps regulate the blood, improve circulation, and improve digestive health.

SWISS MUSHROOM SPINACH OVEN OMELET

An oven omelet is an easy way to serve eggs to your family. I often serve this meal for dinner with toast and hash browns.

2 cups raw baby spinach, packed
3 tablespoons extra-virgin olive oil
4 to 6 mini bella or white mushrooms, sliced
4 eggs
¼ cup milk
1½ cups Swiss cheese, grated
½ teaspoon salt
¼ teaspoon pepper

1. Preheat oven to 350°F. Butter the bottom and sides of an 8 x 8-inch baking dish.
2. In a small frying pan, sauté the spinach in 2 tablespoons olive oil until it is just wilted. Remove from the pan, then place the mushrooms and 1 tablespoon olive oil in the pan. Sauté for 3 to 4 minutes. Spread the mushrooms and spinach evenly in the oven dish.
3. Beat together the eggs, 1 cup cheese, salt, and pepper until smooth. Pour the egg mixture over the vegetables, then sprinkle the rest of the cheese over the top.
4. Bake for 20 minutes, or until eggs are puffy and no longer runny.

Makes 4 servings.

Nutrition Tip: Mushrooms are a good source of potassium and copper. Regularly eating mushrooms can increase your heart health, lower your blood pressure, and strengthen your immune system.

EGG-WHITE OVEN OMELET

A low-calorie, healthy way to eat delicious eggs.

8 egg whites
¼ cup milk or water
¼ teaspoon salt
⅛ teaspoon cracked pepper

1. Preheat oven to 350°F. Lightly butter the bottom and sides of an 8 x 8-inch baking dish.
2. Using an electric mixer on medium to high speed, beat all ingredients together until slightly frothy.
3. Pour the egg mixture into the baking dish. Bake for 30 minutes or until the eggs are set.

For a Southwestern twist, place ¼ cup chopped bell pepper, ¼ cup chopped onion, and 1 teaspoon chopped cilantro in the bottom of the baking dish. Pour the egg mixture over the vegetables. Bake as previously instructed and serve with salsa. If desired, sprinkle ½ cup grated cheese on top before baking.

Makes 4 servings.

LAYERED BISCUIT-BOTTOM BREAKFAST SQUARES

The vegetable layer in these squares can be omitted, making them more like egg and cheese biscuits.

Biscuit Bottom:
1¼ cups flour
1 tablespoon sugar
1 teaspoon baking powder
¼ teaspoon salt
2 tablespoons cold butter
½ cup milk

Egg Layer:
4 eggs
¼ cup milk
1 teaspoon parsley flakes
½ teaspoon salt

¼ teaspoon onion powder
¼ teaspoon pepper
½ cup grated cheddar cheese

Topping:
½ cup grated cheddar cheese

Vegetable Layer (optional):
¼ cup finely chopped onions
¼ cup finely chopped mushrooms
¼ cup sausage substitute crumbles
   (see * on page 123)
¼ cup finely chopped bell pepper

1. Preheat oven to 350°F. Lightly butter the bottom and sides of an 8 x 8-inch baking dish.
2. In a mixing bowl, stir together the flour, sugar, baking powder, and salt.
3. Cut the butter into small chunks, then sprinkle them over the flour mixture. Cut the butter into the flour mixture using two butter knives or a pastry cutter.
4. Stir the milk into the batter. Spread the batter in the bottom of the prepared baking dish.
5. In a small skillet over medium heat, sauté the vegetables and/or vegetarian sausage crumbles in a little olive oil for about 3 minutes. Spread the mixture over the biscuit layer.
6. In a separate bowl, whisk together the egg-layer ingredients until smooth, then pour the mixture over the vegetable layer.
7. Sprinkle the cheese on top and bake for 25 to 30 minutes, or until a toothpick inserted in the center comes out clean. Cut into squares and serve warm or at room temperature.

Makes 6 servings.

SALSA BREAKFAST BURRITO

These breakfast burritos are addictively delicious and satisfying for a hearty appetite!

1 potato, cubed
1¼ cup chopped onion
½ cup vegetable oil
3 large eggs
2 heaping spoonfuls Fresh Salsa (see page 75)
salt and pepper, to taste
½ teaspoon butter
¼ cup grated cheddar cheese
⅓ cup milk
4 tortillas, warmed slightly
Salsa Verde (see page 75)

1. Heat oil in a frying pan over medium-high heat. Add potatoes and onions and fry until crispy, about 5 minutes. Remove potatoes from oil and let drain on paper towels, then season with salt and pepper.
2. In a bowl, stir together eggs, milk, salsa, and a few dashes of salt and pepper. Melt butter in a small frying pan, then add potatoes. Pour egg mixture over potatoes and let cook for about 5 minutes, stirring occasionally, until eggs are fully cooked. Top eggs with cheese. Once cheese is melted, remove pan from heat.
3. Divide the eggs onto the tortillas. Drizzle about 1 tablespoon Salsa Verde onto egg mixture before rolling the tortilla like a burrito.

Makes 4 servings.

Nutrition Tip: Cheese is very high in calcium, protein, and vitamin B. Low-fat cheese is made with skim or reduced-fat milk, so it contains much less saturated fat than regular cheese while still providing the same amount of healthy nutrients. Several brands of organic low-fat cheese, as well as delicious raw cheese, are now available in grocery stores.

SOUTHWEST TOFU BREAKFAST BURRITO

If you've never cooked with tofu, this is a great place to start.
You'll find that it takes on whatever flavors it is cooked with,
and that it has a similar texture to eggs.

¼ cup diced bell pepper
¼ cup diced onions
2 slices firm tofu (about ½ inch thick),
    cut into small cubes
1 tablespoon extra-virgin olive oil
3 eggs
⅓ cup milk
¼ cup cheddar cheese
¼ cup diced tomatoes
4 tortillas
¼ cup Salsa Verde (see page 75)
salt and pepper, to taste

1. In a frying pan, sauté tofu, pepper, and onions in oil for 2 to 3 minutes
2. In a bowl, beat together the eggs, milk, salt, and pepper. Pour the egg mixture over the sautéed mixture and cook, stirring occasionally, until eggs are set. Sprinkle cheese over eggs and let sit until cheese is melted.
3. Top with tomatoes and Salsa Verde. Divide into 4 portions and serve wrapped in warm tortillas.

Makes 4 servings.

❧ MIGAS ❧

This egg dish is traditionally served with fresh hash browns and warm tortillas.

8 large eggs
½ cup milk
½ cup chopped onions
½ cup diced bell pepper
4 tablespoons sliced jalapenos (fresh or bottled)
½ cup grated cheddar or Monterrey Jack cheese
½ cup Fresh Salsa (see page 21)
salt and pepper, to taste
1 cup crumbled tortilla chips
2 teaspoons butter

1. Melt the butter in a small pan over medium heat. Sauté the vegetables in the butter for 2 to 4 minutes.
2. In a small mixing bowl, beat together the eggs and milk. Pour the egg mixture over the vegetables. Stir occasionally until the eggs are set. Top with chips, then cheese, then salsa. Add salt and pepper, to taste.

If Migas with chorizo is a favorite in your home, toss 1 cup vegetarian sausage crumbles or soy chorizo into the egg mixture while cooking. If you like it spicier, just add some Tabasco or Cholula hot sauce.

Makes 4 to 6 servings.

❧PIE CRUST❧

This recipe is to be used in the following four recipes and makes enough dough for three pie crusts. If you are only using one pie crust, divide the remaining dough in half and form into balls, then wrap in plastic wrap and freeze for next time. When you need the dough, just remove it from the freezer and let it sit on the counter for a couple of hours before rolling it out. This versatile dough also makes a delicious crust for any dessert pie.

½ cup butter, softened
⅓ cup shortening
⅓ cup margarine, softened
1 tablespoon sugar
1 tablespoon nonfat dry milk
1 teaspoon salt
½ teaspoon baking powder
1½ cups flour
½ cup cold water

1. Preheat oven to 375°F. Using a hand mixer, cream together the butter, shortening, and margarine in a large mixing bowl. In a small bowl, mix together the sugar, dry milk, salt, and baking powder. Add the dry ingredients (except the flour) to the creamed ingredients, mixing briefly. Add the flour; mix until well blended. Pour in water and mix again. Dough will appear flaky.

2. Combine dough with your hands and divide it into three equal portions. On a lightly floured surface, use a floured rolling pin to roll one of the dough balls into a thin, round crust. Place it in a pie pan and cut off excess dough around the edges. Flute the edges or press with a fork.

3. If your recipe calls for the pie crust to be baked before it is filled, place dried beans or pie-crust weights in the bottom of the crust (to prevent bubbles), then bake for 12 minutes. Before filling the crust with anything, remember to remove the dried beans or pie-crust weights.

Makes 3 pie crusts.

❧ THREE CHEESE QUICHE ❧

*I usually serve this cheesy egg dish at dinnertime
with fresh fruit and muffins.*

1 prepared pie crust, unbaked (see page 21)
5 eggs
½ cup half & half
½ cup grated cheddar cheese
½ cup grated Swiss cheese
½ cup grated Monterrey Jack cheese
½ teaspoon salt
¼ teaspoon cracked pepper

1. Preheat oven to 350°F. In a small mixing bowl, mix the cheeses together.
2. In a medium mixing bowl, use a whisk to beat together the eggs, half & half, salt, pepper, and ½ cup of the cheese mixture.
3. Spread ½ cup cheese mixture on the bottom of the pie crust. Pour egg mixture into the pie crust, then sprinkle the remaining cheese over the top.
4. Bake for 30 minutes or until eggs are puffy and set.

Makes 6 servings.

Nutrition Tip: One hard-boiled egg contains 17 grams of protein. If your only protein source was eggs, you would only need about three per day to meet your body's protein needs.

❧BROCCOLI CHEDDAR QUICHE❧

*This quiche combines delicious flavors of the country with
a bit of sophistication.*

1 uncooked pie crust (see page 21)
4 large eggs
1½ cups puréed broccoli*
1 cup grated cheddar cheese
½ cup milk
¼ cup chopped onions
1 teaspoon salt
½ teaspoon garlic salt
½ teaspoon cracked pepper
⅛ teaspoon cayenne pepper

1. Preheat oven to 375°F. In a mixing bowl, whisk together the eggs, puréed broccoli, ¾ cup grated cheese, milk, onion, and seasonings.
2. Pour the egg mixture into the prepared pie crust, then sprinkle the quiche with the remaining ¼ cup cheese.
3. Bake for 25 to 35 minutes, or until the center of the quiche is set.

*Purée broccoli in a blender or food processor.

Makes 6 servings.

Nutrition Tip: Broccoli is a good source of vitamins A, C, K, and B_9 (folate). This tasty vegetable has anti-inflammatory properties, helps to lower cholesterol, and can reduce the effects of food allergies.

❧PUMPKIN QUICHE❧

This quiche has a delightful, savory flavor that is perfect for fall.

1 prepared pie crust, unbaked (see page 21)
1½ cups cooked puréed pumpkin*
4 eggs
1 cup grated cheddar cheese
⅔ cup half & half
1 tablespoon extra-virgin olive oil
¼ teaspoon salt
¼ teaspoon nutmeg
2 dashes fresh cracked pepper
1 dash ground cloves

1. Preheat oven to 350°F. In a mixing bowl, whisk together pumpkin, eggs, ½ cup cheese, half & half, oil, salt, nutmeg, pepper, and cloves.
2. Pour mixture into pie crust, then sprinkle remaining cheese on top. Bake for 35 to 45 minutes, or until a toothpick inserted in the center comes out clean.

*To roast a pumpkin, cut it into large segments and place it flesh down on a cookie sheet, then bake it for about an hour. It is done when the flesh comes off the skin easily. After the pumpkin flesh has been separated from the skin and cooled, purée it in a food processor. Puréed pumpkin freezes very well in ziptop freezer bags.

Makes 6 servings.

Nutrition Tip: Pumpkin is loaded with beta-carotene, an important antioxidant. During the digestion process, beta-carotene is converted into vitamin A, which is key in fighting off heart disease, certain types of cancers, and other diseases.

❧MINI SPINACH PIES❧

*These pies are the perfect main dish for small dinner parties
and a great way to get your children to love spinach!*

pie dough for 1 pie crust (see page 21)
4 cups baby spinach, packed
1½ cups cubed fresh mozzarella cheese
1 cup ricotta cheese
3 garlic cloves, minced
3 tablespoon extra-virgin olive oil
½ teaspoon salt
¼ teaspoon cracked pepper

1. Preheat oven to 350°F. Divide dough into four pieces and roll it out to fit four 4-inch pie pans. Place dough in pans, then place dried beans in the bottom of each crust to prevent large bubbles from forming. Bake crusts for 10 minutes, then remove the dried beans.

2. In a large frying pan over medium heat, sauté the spinach, oil, and garlic until the spinach begins to wilt.

3. In a medium mixing bowl, gently mix together the cooked spinach, ricotta cheese, mozzarella cubes, and salt and pepper.

4. Fill each pie crust with the spinach pie filling. Bake for 25 minutes.

Makes 4 servings.

❧MINI CHEESE PIZZAS❧

This is a very fun recipe to make with your kids. They will love kneading the dough and decorating the pizzas.

2½ cups flour, plus extra for kneading
1 package rapid-rising yeast
1½ tablespoons flaxseed
½ teaspoon rosemary
2 teaspoons sugar
2½ teaspoons salt
1 cup warm water
2 tablespoons extra-virgin olive oil
1½ cups grated mozzarella cheese
1 cup Zesty Marinara Sauce (see page 145)
    or Fresh Tomato Sauce (see page 143)
additional vegetable toppings, if desired

1. In a large mixing bowl, combine the flour, yeast, flaxseed, rosemary, sugar, and salt. Mix well. Add the water and oil, stirring until a messy dough forms.
2. On a lightly floured surface, knead the dough with floured hands until it is no longer sticky, adding small amounts of flour as needed. Spread a dab of olive oil on the bottom and sides of the mixing bowl, then place the dough back in the bowl and turn it over so that both sides of the dough are oiled. Cover with plastic wrap and let dough rise for 45 to 55 minutes.
3. Separate dough into five equal portions. Form each into a ball, then roll out each ball on a lightly floured surface to form a very thin circle.
4. Spread marinara or tomato sauce on each dough circle. Top with mozzarella cheese, then vegetables (if using).
5. Preheat oven to 450°F and place the oven rack in the lowest position. Line 2 cookie sheets with parchment paper. Place the pizzas on the cookie sheets and bake for 10 to 12 minutes.

Makes 4 servings.

❧PIZZA POCKETS❧

These pockets are amazing—so zesty and full of flavor!

4 cups milk
¼ cup butter
½ cup sugar
1 tablespoon salt
2 eggs, well beaten
2 packages yeast
1 cup warm water
10 cups flour, plus extra as needed

extra-virgin olive oil
2 cups grated mozzarella cheese
½ cup diced onion
½ bell pepper (any color), diced
⅓ cup sliced black olives
2½ cups Zesty Marinara Sauce
   (see page 145)

1. In a saucepan, boil the milk, butter, sugar, and salt. Place the mixture in the fridge for approximately 30 minutes, letting it cool completely.

2. In a large mixing bowl, stir the yeast into the eggs. Add the cooled milk mixture to the egg mixture. Stir in 1 cup of flour at a time. By the eighth or ninth cup, you will need to use your hands. Keep adding flour until the dough is just past the sticky stage. Lift the dough out of the bowl and spread extra-virgin olive oil over the bottom and sides of the mixing bowl. Place the dough back in and then turn it over. Cover the bowl with plastic wrap and let dough rise for 1 hour.

3. While the dough rises, make the filling. In a medium mixing bowl, stir together the cheese, onion, bell pepper, black olives, and marinara sauce. If using softer mozzarella cheese, cut it into small cubes.

4. On a large, lightly floured surface, roll half of the dough into a large rectangle approximately ¼ inch thick. Cut the dough into 4-inch squares.

5. Place 2 to 3 spoonfuls of pizza filling in the center of one square, then fold in each side and pinch the seams together. Repeat the process with each square. Then repeat the entire process with the rest of the dough.

6. Preheat oven to 450°F. Place the pizza pockets 1½ to 2 inches apart on 2 or 3 parchment-lined cookie sheets. Cover each cookie sheet with a thin kitchen towel and let rise 50 minutes. Bake each sheet of risen pizza pockets for 10 to 12 minutes. (Since this recipe makes so much, I freeze the leftovers. To reheat a frozen pizza pocket, bake at 350°F for 35 to 40 minutes.)

Makes 2½ dozen pockets.

❧❧MARGARITA PIZZA❧❧

This basic Italian cheese pizza is absolutely mouthwatering.

Crust:
2½ cups flour
1 cup warm water
1 package yeast
1 teaspoon salt
1 teaspoon sugar
1 teaspoon extra-virgin olive oil

1. Mix flour, salt, sugar, and oil in mixing bowl.
2. In a separate bowl, dissolve yeast in warm water. Combine with flour, kneading mixture until dough is stretchy. Add a little more flour if necessary. Cover with a towel and let rise for 1½ hours.
3. When the dough has risen, stretch it out and work it with your hands into a thin, round crust.

Sauce and Topping:
2 cups peeled and diced tomatoes
1 tablespoon extra-virgin olive oil
1 to 2 garlic cloves, minced
½ teaspoon salt
1 fist-size fresh mozzarella ball*
¼ cup chopped fresh basil

1. Preheat oven to 475°F. Crush the diced tomatoes, with a back of a large spoon, then drain the juice. Stir in the olive oil and salt.
2. Spread the sauce on the crust. Cut the mozzarella into ½-inch thick slices. Arrange the mozzarella slices on the sauce, then sprinkle the basil on top.
3. Bake for 10 minutes or until cheese is bubbly.

*Fresh mozzarella balls are soft, stored in water, and can be found next to the imported cheeses at the grocery store.

Makes 1 pizza.

❧ROASTED MUSHROOM PIZZA❧

If you don't have a cooking stone, use a parchment-lined baking pan.

Crust:
1 cup all-purpose flour
1½ tablespoons extra-virgin olive oil
1 teaspoon sea salt
1½ tablespoons agave nectar

Topping:
Zesty Marinara Sauce (see page 145)
2 fist-size balls of soft mozzarella
1 to 2 cups sliced mushrooms
extra-virgin olive oil
sea salt

1. Let the yeast sit in the warm water for about 10 minutes, or until it dissolves. (It will turn foamy on top.)
2. In a large mixing bowl, stir together all of the ingredients. Knead with your hands until all of the flour is incorporated into the dough. Lift up the dough, put a dab of olive oil in the bowl, then rub the oil around the bottom and sides of the bowl with your fingers. Place the dough back in the bowl, then turn the dough over to oil both sides. Cover with plastic wrap and let rise, at room temperature, for about 45 minutes.
3. Preheat oven to 400°F. Spread the mushroom slices on a cookie sheet, then drizzle them with olive oil and sprinkle them with sea salt. Stir the mushrooms to coat them in oil and salt. Bake for 5 to 10 minutes, then set aside.
4. Lower oven temperature to 325°F. On a lightly floured surface, roll out the dough into a very large circle. (If you want to make two 10- to 12-inch pizzas, cut the dough in half and roll out each piece.)
5. Spread the Zesty Marinara Sauce on the dough. Slice the mozzarella balls and place the slices on the sauce. Sprinkle the roasted mushrooms over the cheese.
6. Bake the pizza for 20 to 30 minutes, or until all of the cheese is melted and the crust is golden brown.

Makes 1 pizza.

❧EGG AND CHEESE KOLACHES❧

From the Czech Republic, kolaches are sweet bread rolls that are filled, usually with fruit. These kolaches make a satisfying, convenient breakfast food.

Dough:
1 package yeast
1 cup warm water
2 cups flour
1½ tablespoons extra-virgin olive oil
1½ tablespoons agave nectar
1 teaspoon sea salt

Filling:
4 eggs
½ cup grated cheese
¼ cup milk
¼ teaspoon sea salt
⅛ teaspoon cracked pepper

1. Lightly butter the bottom and sides of a 9 x 13-inch baking dish. Set aside.

2. In a large bowl, stir together the warm water and yeast. Let stand for about 10 minutes, or until the mixture is foamy.

3. Stir in the flour, olive oil, agave nectar, and salt. Knead the mixture until all of the flour is incorporated into the dough. Lift the dough from the bowl, spread a dab of oil over the bottom and sides of the bowl, return the dough to the bowl, and then turn it over to oil both sides. Cover the bowl with plastic wrap and let rise for 1 hour to 1 hour and 15 minutes.

4. When the dough has almost finished rising, make the filling. In a bowl, beat together the eggs, milk, salt, and pepper. Cook the egg mixture in a skillet over medium heat, stirring occasionally, until the eggs are set. Stir the cheese in while the eggs are still cooking.

5. Divide the dough into 12 equal balls (by dividing in half, then dividing the two halves in half, and so on). On a lightly floured surface, roll out each ball, then place about 3 tablespoons of filling in the middle of the rolled-out dough.

6. Tuck the edges of the dough over and around the filling, then pinch the edges together, covering the filling completely with the dough. Put the kolaches into the prepared baking dish, making four rows of three. Cover with plastic and let rise for another 45 to 60 minutes.

7. Preheat oven to 325°F. Bake kolaches for 30 to 35 minutes, or until they turn a nice golden brown. Remove from the oven, then brush with butter.

Makes 12 kolaches.

✣THREE-CHEESE STUFFED MUSHROOMS✣

Serve these tasty goodies as an appetizer, a side dish, or a main dish.

18 mini bella mushrooms
1 cup ricotta cheese
½ cup grated mozzarella cheese
⅓ cup grated Parmesan cheese
2 garlic cloves, minced
¼ teaspoon salt
⅛ teaspoon cracked pepper
3 tablespoons butter, melted
⅓ cup breadcrumbs
2 dashes garlic salt
3 dashes dried basil

1. Preheat oven to 400°F. Remove the mushroom stems and place the mushrooms in a single layer in an 8 x 8-inch baking dish, with the bottom side up.
2. Using a fork, mash together the cheeses, garlic, salt, and pepper. Place about 1 tablespoon of this stuffing into and on top of each mushroom cap.
3. Make the topping by melting the butter then stirring the breadcrumbs, garlic salt, and basil into the crumb mixture. With your fingers, gently press about 1 teaspoon topping onto the stuffing in each mushroom cap.
4. Bake for 13 to 15 minutes, or until the crumbs are golden brown and the cheese is slightly bubbly.

Makes 6 to 8 servings.

Nutrition Tip: Garlic contains surprisingly large amounts of protein, vitamin C, calcium, iron, and magnesium.

BROCCOLI CHEESE SOUP

If you want to make an easy but delicious meal and don't know where to start, look no further. You probably have these simple ingredients on hand.

4 cups milk

two 12-ounce cans cream of broccoli soup

2 cups grated cheddar cheese

2 cups chopped frozen broccoli

3 teaspoons mustard

½ teaspoon salt

4 to 6 dashes fresh cracked pepper

Mix all ingredients in a stockpot. Cook at medium heat for about 20 minutes, stirring occasionally.

Makes 4 to 6 servings.

Cooking Method: Buttered Broccoli

In a covered saucepan over medium heat, place broccoli florets in a little water seasoned with butter and salt (for 2 cups broccoli florets, I use ⅓ cup water, 2 tablespoons butter, and ½ teaspoon salt). Cook for 10 minutes, or until broccoli is tender but not limp.

CAJUN DEVILED EGGS

With a smooth and slightly spicy filling, these eggs taste heavenly.

6 hard-boiled eggs, peeled
1 tablespoon grated celery pulp
1 tablespoon grated onion pulp
¼ teaspoon Tony Chachere's Original Creole Seasoning
2 dashes fresh cracked pepper
1 teaspoon mustard
1 teaspoon canola mayonnaise
½ teaspoon relish
paprika

1. Cut eggs in half lengthwise. Put the yolks in a mixing bowl, and place the empty egg whites hole side up on a plate.
2. Mash the yolks, then stir in the remaining ingredients except the paprika. Gently scoop the yolk mixture into the hole in each egg white. Sprinkle each egg half with a little paprika.

Makes 6 servings.

Nutrition Tip: Celery is an excellent source of vitamin C, which boosts the immune system and helps prevent and reduce symptoms of the common cold.

CREAM CHEESE WONTONS

These wontons are the perfect compliment to any Asian meal. Or try serving the wontons with vegetables for a delightful main course.

24 round wonton wraps
vegetable oil
8-ounce package cream cheese, at room temperature
3 garlic cloves, minced
3 tablespoons chopped chives
spring roll dipping sauce*

1. Pour vegetable oil in a frying pan until it is about ½ inch deep. Heat over medium heat.

2. Combine cream cheese, garlic, and chives. Stir together until smooth. Place about 1 tablespoon of the cream-cheese mixture in the center of each wonton wrap. With wet fingers, fold wrap in half and press firmly along sides to seal closed. Do not stack the wontons; make a single layer on a plate and let dry for about 5 minutes.

3. Place wontons in the heated oil in a single layer, only cooking about 6 at a time. Cook for about 4 minutes on each side. Wrap will be bubbly and slightly crispy when it is done. Remove from oil and drain on paper towels before serving. Serve with dipping sauce on the side.

*Spring roll dipping sauce may be found in the Asian food aisle of most grocery stores. Duck sauce or sweet and sour sauce may be substituted.

Makes 6 servings.

SPINACH ARTICHOKE MUSHROOM DIP

This dip is a party favorite. For a large crowd, double the recipe and use a 9 x 13-inch baking dish.

1½ cups chopped fresh spinach
2 garlic cloves, minced
2 tablespoons extra-virgin olive oil
14-ounce can artichoke hearts, drained and chopped
2 large mushrooms, chopped
8-ounce package cream cheese, at room temperature
½ cup sour cream
½ cup Parmesan cheese
¼ cup canola mayonnaise
½ teaspoon salt
¼ teaspoon garlic salt
¼ teaspoon crushed red pepper
⅛ teaspoon cracked pepper

1. Preheat oven to 350°F. In a frying pan over medium heat, sauté the spinach and garlic in the oil until spinach is just wilted.
2. In an 8 x 8-inch baking dish, combine the spinach mixture with the remaining ingredients, reserving ¼ cup Parmesan cheese. Stir together well, then spread out evenly. Sprinkle remaining cheese on top, then bake for 25 minutes.
3. Serve with pita chips, toasted sourdough baguette slices, or whole-grain crackers.

Makes 6 to 8 servings.

QUESADILLAS

This is a popular meal at our house. It's so quick and easy to make, and it satisfies a hungry appetite!

8 tortillas
1⅓ cup grated cheddar cheese
butter
sour cream, Easy Guacamole (see page 65),
   and/or Fresh Salsa (see page 75)
1 cup chopped onions and green bell pepper (optional)

1. Heat griddle or large frying pan and lightly coat with butter.
2. Place 1 tortilla on the heated surface, then cover tortilla with ⅓ cup cheese. Press another tortilla on top of the cheese. If you are using onions and peppers, place about ¼ cup on top of the cheese, then sprinkle on a little more cheese. Cover with the second tortilla. After about 2 minutes, when cheese begins to melt, flip the quesadilla over and cook for another 2 minutes. Repeat the entire process for the remaining tortillas.
3. Remove from heat and cut like pizza slices. Serve with guacamole, sour cream, and/or salsa on the side.

Makes 4 servings.

❧STUFFED JALAPENOS❧

*In this addictive dish, the cheese and lime juice
tame the heat of the jalapenos.*

6 jalapenos
8-ounce package cream cheese, at room temperature
¼ cup grated Monterrey Jack cheese
juice from 1 lime
¼ teaspoon salt
1 tablespoon butter
¼ cup breadcrumbs

1. Preheat oven to 350°F. Cut the jalapenos in half lengthwise, then remove the stems and seeds. Place jalapenos on a cookie sheet.
2. In a mixing bowl, use a fork to mash together the cream cheese, Monterrey Jack cheese, lime juice, and salt. Place equal amounts of the cheese filling in the jalapeno halves.
3. Melt the butter and stir in the breadcrumbs. Spread and gently press down equal amounts of the breadcrumb mixture on top of the stuffed jalapenos.
4. Bake for 22 to 25 minutes, until the jalapenos have reached the desired tenderness and breadcrumbs are golden brown.

Makes 6 servings.

Nutrition Tip: Jalapenos are famous for clearing congestion. They can also help alleviate migraines and sinus headaches.

CREAM CHEESE TAQUITOS

These taquitos are soft on the inside and crunchy on the outside.

8-ounce package cream cheese, at room temperature*
4-ounce can diced green chilies
¼ cup canola oil
10 to 12 corn tortillas
Fresh Salsa (see page 75) and/or Easy Guacamole
    (see page 65) for dipping

1. Preheat oven to 400°F. Heat the oil in a small frying pan over medium heat.
2. In a mixing bowl, use a fork to mash together the cream cheese and chilies.
3. Using a fork or tongs, dip a corn tortilla in the heated oil for about 10 seconds on each side. Place the dipped tortilla on a cookie sheet. Use your fingers to put 2 or 3 tablespoons cream cheese down the center of the tortilla. Quickly fold and tuck in the sides of the tortilla to make a long, burrito-like shape. Repeat the process until all ingredients are used.
4. Place taquitos side by side on the cookie sheet. Bake for 6 to 8 minutes. Serve warm.

* If you need a dairy-free alternative to cream cheese, my favorite is Better Than Cream Cheese by Tofutti™. The taste and texture are exactly like regular cream cheese; if you didn't know you were eating dairy free, you wouldn't notice the difference.

Makes 6 to 8 servings.

Nutrition Tip: Canola oil is low in cholesterol and contains significant amounts of vitamin E and vitamin K. It is very low in saturated fat and contains omega-3 and omega-6 essential fatty acids. Canola oil is one of the healthier cooking oils, along with extra-virgin olive oil and coconut oil, among others.

CHEESE ENCHILADAS

*If your family likes TexMex food, they will love this dish.
I serve these enchiladas with Spanish Rice (see page 117)
and Cuban Black Beans (see page 105).*

12 to 14 corn tortillas
28-ounce can diced tomatoes
¼ cup chopped onions
2 garlic cloves, minced
1 tablespoon Cholula hot sauce
½ teaspoon salt
¼ cup canola oil
¼ teaspoon chili powder

¼ teaspoon cumin
¼ teaspoon pepper
½ teaspoon oregano
1 cup grated cheddar cheese, packed
1 cup grated Monterrey Jack, packed
2 cups shredded lettuce
sour cream (optional)

1. Preheat oven to 350°F. In a large frying pan, sauté the onions, garlic, and dried spices in oil for 3 to 5 minutes, then add the hot sauce and canned tomatoes. Cook over medium heat for another 7 to 10 minutes.

2. Spread 1 cup of the sauce in a 9 x 13-inch baking dish. Combine the cheeses in a mixing bowl.

3. Leave the remaining sauce on the stove to keep warm. Place a tortilla in the sauce for a few seconds on each side (you want the tortilla to be flexible and moist but not soggy). Then place 2 to 3 heaping spoonfuls of the cheese mixture down the center of the tortilla. Roll the tortilla and place it in the baking dish. Repeat the process, placing the enchiladas side by side in a single layer in the dish.

4. Pour the remaining sauce evenly over the enchiladas, then sprinkle the remaining cheese on top.

5. Bake for 20 minutes or until all the cheese is melted. Place a small dollop of sour cream on each portion, if desired.

Makes 6 servings.

CREAM-CHEESE AND CORN ENCHILADAS

These enchiladas taste absolutely heavenly. Make them once and your family will be hooked.

1 package corn or flour tortillas
enchilada salsa
cheese filling
½ cup grated cheddar cheese

Enchilada Salsa:
1 tomato

1 green bell pepper, stem and seeds removed
¼ onion
1 garlic clove, peeled
½ jalapeno, seeded
3 tablespoons cilantro
1 teaspoon Cholula hot sauce
½ teaspoon salt

Purée all ingredients together in a blender or food processor.

Cheese Filling:
12 ounces cream cheese, at room
    temperature
1 cup frozen corn, defrosted
2 garlic cloves, minced

1 cup grated Monterrey Jack cheese
¼ teaspoon salt
⅛ teaspoon cracked pepper

Using a fork, mash all ingredients together in a bowl.

Directions for making enchiladas:

1. Preheat oven to 350°F. Spread about ¼ of the salsa in a 9 x 13-inch baking dish.
2. Heat the remaining salsa in a frying pan over medium-low heat, then soak tortillas, one at a time, in the hot salsa for a few seconds on each side (the tortillas should be flexible but not soggy).
3. Place 3 to 4 tablespoons cheese filling down the middle of each soaked tortilla. Roll up the tortilla and place it in the oven dish with the folded edges down. Repeat the process with each tortilla, placing them in a tight single layer in the baking dish.
4. Spread the rest of the salsa over the enchiladas, then sprinkle cheddar cheese over the top. Bake enchiladas for about 30 minutes or until all cheese is melted.

Makes 6 to 8 servings.

SOUR CREAM AND ONION CHEESE BALL

This appetizer has an addictive flavor.

8-ounce package cream cheese, at room temperature
2 tablespoons sour cream
2 tablespoons onion pulp*
¼ teaspoon salt
¼ teaspoon garlic salt
¼ teaspoon onion powder
¾ teaspoon parsley flakes
2 tablespoons chopped chives

1. In a small mixing bowl, combine the cream cheese, sour cream, onion pulp, salt, garlic salt, onion powder, ¼ teaspoon parsley, and 1 tablespoon chives. Work the mixture into a ball with your hands.
2. In another bowl, combine 1 tablespoon chives and ½ teaspoon parsley, then use your fingers to gently press the mixture into the outside of the cheese ball.
3. Serve with a small spreading knife in the center and an arrangement of crackers, pretzels, and cut vegetables such as carrots and celery.

*To make onion pulp, rub the open side of an onion back and forth over a cheese grater.

Makes 1 cheese ball.

Nutrition Tip: It is a well-known fact that eating carrots can improve eye health. Carrots can also strengthen the immune system, dispel congestion, prevent acne, and reduce cancer risks.

❧BAKED CHEESE FONDUE❧

Spread this delicious fondue on sliced French bread.

2 cups grated Swiss cheese
2 eggs
½ cup milk
1 tablespoon butter, at room temperature
1 tablespoon Dijon mustard
¼ teaspoon salt
⅛ teaspoon cracked pepper
dash of nutmeg

1. Preheat oven to 350°F. Lightly butter the bottom and sides of an 8 x 8-inch baking dish.
2. Using an electric mixer, beat all ingredients together until light and bubbly. This should take less than 1 minute on high speed.
3. Pour mixture into prepared dish and bake for 40 to 50 minutes. The finished product will be slightly puffy, and the eggs will be set, not runny.

Makes 6 to 8 servings.

Nutrition Tip: Nutmeg contains antibacterial properties, helps to improve memory, and aids in digestion.

FRUIT AND
VEGETABLE DISHES

CHICKPEA, BROCCOLI, AND QUINOA CASSEROLE

This fabulous casserole is full of protein, calcium, iron, fiber, and carbohydrates.

1½ cups cooked chickpeas (if using canned, drain and rinse them)
1 cup quinoa, uncooked
2 cups water
2 cups chopped broccoli
½ cup sour cream
1 cup milk
1 cup grated cheese
2 garlic cloves, minced
¼ cup chopped onion
1 teaspoon sea salt
1 teaspoon garlic salt
¼ teaspoon pepper

1. Preheat oven to 350°F. In a bowl of water, soak the dry quinoa for about 15 minutes. Drain off and discard the soaking water. Steam the quinoa in 2 cups of water. If the quinoa is not tender enough when the water has cooked out, add a bit more water, cover again, and steam until the quinoa is soft.
2. Steam the broccoli for about 5 minutes in a small, covered pan.
3. In a 2-quart casserole dish, stir together the chickpeas, steamed quinoa, steamed broccoli, sour cream, milk, ¾ cup grated cheese, garlic, onion, and seasonings.
4. Spread the mixture evenly in the baking dish. Sprinkle the remaining cheese on top. Bake casserole for 20 to 25 minutes.

Makes 6 servings.

GRILLED VEGGIE KEBOBS

A friend of mine invited me to a barbecue, then apologized when she remembered I am a vegetarian. I told her I would love to come and that I would bring something to grill. These kebobs were a hit!

1 red sweet pepper
1 green bell pepper
1 purple onion
1 cup fresh pineapple chunks
1 cup grape tomatoes
Basic Kebob Marinade (see below)

1. Cut the peppers and onion into large chunks. Place in a mixing bowl with the pineapple and tomatoes. Pour the marinade over the pineapple and vegetables, then stir, cover, and let marinate for at least 20 minutes.
2. Using your own pattern to make a colorful presentation, skewer fruits and vegetables. Grill them on a low setting for 15 to 20 minutes or until the vegetables reach the desired tenderness. Turn kebobs at least once while cooking.

Makes 4 to 5 servings.

BASIC KEBOB MARINADE

½ cup extra-virgin olive oil
1 teaspoon honey
½ teaspoon oregano
½ teaspoon salt

In a mixing bowl, stir ingredients together with a wire whisk.

Makes ½ cup.

❧ VEGAN GARDEN BURGER PATTIES ❧

Sometimes you just need a burger! Keep these patties in your freezer so you can easily satisfy those cravings.

¾ cup wild field rice

1½ cups water

1 large portabella mushroom

1½ cups cooked kidney beans (if using canned, drain and rinse them)

¼ onion

3 to 4 garlic cloves, peeled

1 celery rib

1 carrot, peeled

¾ cup water

1 teaspoon sea salt

1 teaspoon garlic salt

1 teaspoon parsley flakes

½ teaspoon onion powder

¼ teaspoon ground cumin

¼ teaspoon cracked pepper

¼ cup whole-wheat flour

¼ cup flax meal

1. In a covered saucepan, steam the wild rice in 1½ cups water (if the water cooks out and the rice isn't soft yet, add a little more water, then cover and cook a little longer).

2. In a food processor, chop and blend the steamed rice, portabella mushroom, kidney beans, onion, garlic, celery, carrot, and ¾ cup water until the mixture is only slightly chunky. Transfer the mixture to a mixing bowl, then stir in the remaining ingredients.

3. Heat a lightly oiled large skillet or griddle to medium or 300°F. Scoop about ⅓ cup burger batter onto the hot surface and gently press down in the middle with a spatula. Repeat this process for each desired patty. After cooking about 3 minutes, turn the patties over (you might need to lightly oil the surface again), and cook for another 3 to 4 minutes.

4. To freeze patties for future meals, line 1 to 2 cookie sheets with parchment paper. Form individual patties on the paper with the raw batter. Freeze the cookie sheets until the patties are firm, then transfer the patties into a freezable storage bag. When you remove the patties from the freezer, there is no need to defrost them; simply add a couple of minutes to the cooking time.

Makes 10 to 12 patties.

BRUSCHETTA

This simple meal is popular on hot summer evenings in Italy. Unlike the bruschetta served at many Italian restaurants in the United States, authentic bruschetta is not baked or broiled.

4 slices of French bread, about 1 inch thick
1 Roma tomato, diced
2 teaspoons extra-virgin olive oil
4 dashes dried basil
salt and pepper, to taste

Arrange tomato pieces on the slices of bread, then drizzle ½ teaspoon olive oil on each slice. Sprinkle a dash of basil on each slice, then add salt and pepper, to taste.

Makes 2 to 4 servings.

Nutrition Tip: The antioxidants found in tomatoes help prevent several types of cancer, including colon, prostate, breast, endometrial, lung, and pancreatic.

❦CUCUMBER SANDWICHES❦

These sandwiches are quick and refreshing. As a meal, I serve three or four of them per person.

potato rolls
Roma tomatoes, sliced
cucumber, sliced
Swiss cheese, sliced
canola mayonnaise
mustard
salt and pepper

Cut the desired number of potato rolls in half to make sandwiches. On the inside of each half, spread a little mustard and canola mayo. Then sprinkle with salt and pepper, to taste. Add a slice of Swiss cheese, a slice of tomato, and 2 slices of cucumber, then top with the other half of the bun.

Nutrition Tip: Cucumbers are a good source of vitamin A, vitamin C, potassium, folate, and fiber.

❧SPRING ROLLS❧

Homemade spring rolls taste so fresh and crisp. These are perfect with almost any type of Asian meal.

6 to 7 large Chinese cabbage leaves
2 carrots, peeled
2 mushrooms
½ teaspoon salt
¼ teaspoon cracked pepper
11 to 13 eggroll wrappers
canola oil
spring roll dipping sauce*

1. Pour canola oil into a frying pan until it is ¼ inch deep, then heat over medium heat.
2. Place the cabbage, carrots, and mushrooms in a food processor and shred them (5 to 8 pulses). Stir in the salt and pepper.
3. Place 2 to 3 tablespoons of the vegetable mixture down the center of a wrapper. Then fold the wrapper according to package instructions, using wet fingers to close and seal the spring roll.
4. Place the roll in the heated oil and cook on both sides until golden brown and bubbly, about 4 to 5 minutes. Allow rolls to dry on paper towels. Serve with spring roll dipping sauce on the side.

*Spring roll dipping sauce is commonly found in the Asian food aisle of a grocery store. Duck sauce or sweet and sour sauce is a good substitute.

Makes 5 to 6 servings.

CHINESE CASHEW VEGETABLE STIR-FRY

If you've never made Chinese food, try this recipe and see how easy it is.

4 mushrooms
4 garlic cloves, peeled
⅔ cup raw cashew nuts
2 tablespoons sesame oil
½ cup soy sauce
2 tablespoons vinegar
4 teaspoons sugar
½ teaspoon crushed red pepper
4 heaping cups broccoli florets
2 carrots, thinly sliced
1 cup green peas (frozen are okay)
10 leaves Chinese cabbage, shredded

1. Purée mushrooms and garlic in a blender or food processor.
2. In a large pan, heat the oil over medium heat. Add the cashews and cook for 2 to 3 minutes, stirring constantly.
3. Add the mushroom mixture and cook for 1 minute.
4. Stir in the remaining ingredients except the peas and cabbage. Cook for 5 to 7 minutes.
5. Add the peas and cabbage and cook for another 5 to 7 minutes. Serve alone or over steamed rice.

Makes 4 to 6 servings.

Nutrition Tip: Eating sesame seeds can help relieve pain and swelling from rheumatoid arthritis, along with helping promote vascular and respiratory health.

❧ MINESTRONE ❧

You'll love the zesty Italian flavor of this soul-filling soup.

2 tablespoons chopped onions
2 garlic cloves, minced
2 tablespoons extra-virgin olive oil
2 cans vegetable broth
3 cups water
15-ounce can kidney beans (do not drain)
6-ounce can tomato paste
1 large potato, cubed
1 large carrot, sliced
1 small zucchini, sliced
1 small yellow squash, sliced
2 celery stalks, sliced
1 cup green beans (fresh or frozen)
1 cup penne pasta
½ cup frozen vegetarian sausage crumbles (optional)
1 teaspoon sea salt
1 teaspoon garlic salt
½ teaspoon onion powder
¼ teaspoon cracked pepper
¼ teaspoon dried basil
Parmesan cheese, shredded (optional)

1. In a large stockpot, sauté the onions and garlic in oil for 2 to 4 minutes.
2. Add the vegetable broth, water, tomato paste, potato cubes, carrots, and seasonings. Boil until the potatoes are tender (20 to 30 minutes), then add the remaining ingredients and cook another 10 to 12 minutes. The soup is done when the pasta is tender.
3. If desired, sprinkle a little Parmesan cheese on each serving.

Makes 6 servings.

Nutrition Tip: Steamed green beans contain substantial amounts of vitamin A, vitamin C, and folate.

CREAM OF CAULIFLOWER AND POTATO SOUP

Any cooked beans or mixed frozen vegetables would be excellent additions to this soup. Just stir in while it is cooking.

½ head of cauliflower
1 large potato, peeled and cut in half or thirds
4 cups water
1½ cups vegetable broth
1 cup milk (or rice milk)
¼ cup chopped onions
3 garlic cloves, minced
2 tablespoons extra-virgin olive oil
1½ teaspoons salt
1½ teaspoons garlic salt
¼ teaspoon cracked pepper
¼ teaspoon crushed red pepper
1 cup grated cheese (your favorite variety)

1. Cut the cauliflower into large chunks. In a stockpot, stir together all ingredients except the cheese. Cook over medium heat for 20 to 25 minutes.
2. When the potato and cauliflower pieces are soft, remove them from the soup with a slotted spoon. Purée the cauliflower and potato in a blender or food processor, then return them to the soup.
3. Stir in the grated cheese and continue to cook and stir the soup until the cheese is fully incorporated.

Makes 8 servings.

CREAMY VEGETABLE QUINOA SOUP

Quinoa in an excellent vegan protein source.

5 cups water
3 cups vegetable broth
1 cup milk (or rice milk)
1 large potato, peeled and cut in half or thirds
2 carrots, sliced
1 cup green beans (frozen or fresh)
2 celery ribs, sliced
1 small yellow squash, sliced
½ cup diced radishes
2 tablespoons chopped fresh parsley or cilantro
½ cup quinoa, uncooked
1 tablespoon extra-virgin olive oil
1½ teaspoons salt
1 teaspoon garlic powder
1 teaspoon onion powder
¼ teaspoon cracked pepper

1. In a stockpot over medium heat, stir all ingredients together. Cover the soup and let cook for about 25 to 30 minutes, stirring occasionally.
2. Remove the large potato pieces and mash them in a separate bowl with a bit of the liquid from the soup. Return the mashed potato to the soup, stir, and let cook another 5 minutes.

Makes 10 servings.

Cooking Method: French Green Beans

In a saucepan, combine 2 cups raw French-style green beans (haricots vert), ½ cup water, 2 tablespoons olive oil, ½ teaspoon salt, ¼ teaspoon cracked pepper, and a dash of garlic salt. Cover pan and steam over medium heat until beans are tender but not limp, about 10 minutes. Makes 4 to 5 servings.

CREAMY BUTTERNUT SQUASH SOUP

This warm and comforting soup gets lapped up quickly at my house.
I like to serve it with hot, whole-grain rolls.

2- to 3-pound butternut squash
2 cups water
2 cans vegetable broth
1 cup half & half
1 onion, chopped
2 tablespoons butter
¾ teaspoon salt
¼ teaspoon nutmeg
¼ teaspoon cracked pepper

1. Peel the butternut squash, remove the seeds, and cut the flesh into small chunks.
2. In a stockpot over medium heat, sauté onions in butter for 3 to 5 minutes. Add remaining ingredients. Cover and cook for 35 to 40 minutes, stirring occasionally.
3. With a large, slotted spoon, remove squash chunks, then purée in a food processor. Return squash to the soup and simmer for 10 minutes.

Makes 6 servings.

❧HEARTY VEGETABLE SOUP❧

*If you do not have all of these vegetables, that is fine. Just use
ten to twelve cups of a large variety of vegetables.*

10 cups water
1 can vegetable broth
1 potato, peeled and diced
1 carrot, peeled and sliced
1 celery stalk, sliced
2 or 3 garlic cloves, sliced
1 cup Fresh Tomato Sauce (see page 143)
½ cup chopped onion
1 small zucchini, sliced
½ small yellow squash, sliced
1 cup frozen green peas
1 cup kidney beans (if using canned, drain and rinse them)
1 cup frozen green beans
1 cup broccoli florets
1 cup cauliflower florets
2 or 3 mushrooms, sliced
3 tablespoons extra-virgin olive oil
1½ teaspoons salt
1½ teaspoons garlic salt
1 teaspoon dried basil
1 teaspoon oregano flakes
½ teaspoon pepper
1 cup pasta, any shape

1. Heat the water and broth in a stockpot over medium-high heat. Add the potatoes and carrots first, then gradually add the rest of the ingredients except the pasta. Cook for 30 to 40 minutes, stirring occasionally, until all of the vegetables are tender.
2. Add the pasta and let cook for another 10 minutes, or until the pasta is tender.

Makes 8 servings.

BAKED POTATO SOUP

This soup is thick, hearty, and delicious.

4 potatoes, peeled and diced
1 can vegetable broth
1 cup milk
3 cups water
¼ cup chopped onion
1½ cups grated cheddar cheese
2 tablespoons butter
1½ teaspoons salt
⅓ teaspoons pepper
¼ teaspoons dried parsley
sour cream
chives

1. Place the potatoes, broth, milk, water, onions, 1 cup cheese, butter, and seasonings in a stockpot. Cook for 30 minutes over medium-high heat, then use a potato masher to mash the soft potatoes in the soup to make it extra creamy. Cook soup for another 5 to 15 minutes.
2. To serve, place the soup in soup bowls, then top with the desired amount of grated cheddar cheese, sour cream, and chives, to be stirred in by each person.

Makes 6 servings.

❧ITALIAN TOMATO SOUP❧

This soup is very satisfying as is, but my children like it when I add tiny pasta stars.

5 large tomatoes, puréed
1 can vegetable broth
1½ cups milk
1 cup water
2½ tablespoons extra-virgin olive oil
1½ teaspoons dried basil
1 teaspoon salt
1 teaspoon garlic salt
1 teaspoon onion powder
¼ teaspoon cracked pepper
1 cup shredded Parmesan cheese

1. Place all ingredients except Parmesan cheese in a stockpot, then cook over medium heat for 20 to 25 minutes, stirring occasionally. Add the cheese during the last 10 minutes of cooking and stir until it is melted and evenly incorporated.
2. If you want to add pasta to the soup (orzo would work nicely), add 1 cup just after the cheese has dissolved, then cook another 10 minutes.

Makes 4 servings.

Nutrition Tip: The omega fatty acids found in extra-virgin olive oil (as well as legumes, flaxseed, spinach, almonds, and kiwifruit) help prevent heart disease, strokes, and learning disabilities, as well as attention-deficit hyperactivity disorder in children.

SPINACH MUSHROOM RAG SOUP

This is a great way to use extra lasagna noodles.

6 to 7 lasagna noodles
2 to 3 cups chopped fresh spinach, packed
4 to 5 mushrooms, diced
3 garlic cloves, minced
¼ cup chopped onions
3 tablespoons extra-virgin olive oil
1½ cups milk
3 cups vegetable broth
1½ cups water
1 teaspoon sea salt
1 teaspoon garlic salt
1 teaspoon dried basil
¼ cracked pepper
1 cup grated mozzarella cheese
¼ cup grated Parmesan cheese, plus extra for topping

1. In a large stockpot over medium heat, sauté the spinach, mushrooms, garlic, and onions until the spinach is just wilted. Stir in the liquids and seasonings.
2. Once the mixture is boiling, break up the lasagna noodles and stir them into the pot.
3. After about 10 minutes, when the noodles are cooked, stir in the mozzarella and Parmesan cheeses. The soup is ready to serve when the cheese is melted and blended into the soup. (Avoid clumps by stirring constantly and scraping the bottom of the pot frequently for a few minutes after adding the cheese.)

Makes 6 servings.

✦VEGETARIAN BORSCHT✦

*A deep reddish-purple soup with Ukrainian origins, borscht is
a fabulous way to use vegetables from the garden.*

3 quarts water
1 large potato, peeled
1½ cups cooked kidney beans
2 carrots, peeled and sliced
1 cup shredded cabbage
3 celery ribs, sliced
4 to 6 mushrooms, diced
1 to 2 large beets, peeled and diced
¼ cup chopped onion
3 garlic cloves, minced
2 teaspoons sea salt
½ cup sour cream
1 tablespoon red wine vinegar

1. In a stockpot over medium heat, stir all ingredients together except the sour cream and vinegar. Leave the potato whole or cut it in half. Stirring occasionally, cook until all of the vegetables (including the potato) are tender.
2. Remove the potato from the soup and place it in a bowl. Mash the potato with the sour cream and vinegar, then stir the mixture into the soup. Cook another 5 minutes before serving.

Makes 6 to 8 servings.

Nutrition Tip: Beans are high in folic acid, which helps fight off lung and pancreatic cancer.

❧EASY COUNTRY VEGETABLE POT PIE❧

This recipe is simple because the crust is made of ready-made crescent-roll dough. Pie crust dough also works well (see page 21).

two 8-ounce packages crescent-roll
  dough
1 large potato, peeled and cubed
½ onion, chopped
2 carrots, peeled and sliced
2 celery stalks, sliced
1 cup frozen green peas

½ cup frozen corn
1 cup broccoli, chopped
3 vegetable bouillon cubes
6 cups water
½ cup flour
1½ teaspoons salt
¼ teaspoon pepper

1. Divide dough into two portions. Using a rolling pin, roll out one portion of dough on a lightly floured surface to fit a 9-inch pie pan. Line the bottom and sides of the pan with the dough. Roll out the other piece of dough and reserve for the top crust of the pie. Set crusts aside.

2. Place the water, vegetables, bouillon cubes, and ½ teaspoon salt in a large pot, then bring to a boil. Cover and let simmer until potatoes and carrots are tender (about 30 minutes). Remove vegetables from pot; place in a bowl and set aside.

3. In a small mixing bowl, combine flour, 1 teaspoon salt, and ½ cup broth, stirring with a whisk until smooth.

4. In a large saucepan, bring 3 cups broth to boil, then whisk in the flour mixture. Cook and stir for 2 minutes until thick. Remove from heat and stir in vegetables.

5. Pour vegetable mixture into dough-lined pie pan. Place remaining crust on top; cut off excess and flute the edges. Cover the edges of the pie with foil and cut 2 or 3 slits in the top. Place the pie on a cookie sheet.

6. Bake at 400°F for 25 minutes, then remove the foil and bake for another 5 minutes.

Makes 6 servings.

CHUNKY VEGETABLE GRAVY AND POTATOES

This savory meal will definitely stick to your ribs.

4 potatoes
2 tablespoons extra-virgin olive oil
½ cup chopped onions
1 cup broccoli florets
1 cup cauliflower florets
1 carrot, peeled and sliced
1 can kidney beans, drained and rinsed
1 can cream of mushroom soup
2 cans milk
½ cup grated cheddar cheese
1 teaspoon sea salt
1 teaspoon garlic salt
½ teaspoon dried parsley
¼ teaspoon cracked pepper

1. Wrap the potatoes in foil and bake at 350°F for an hour, or until they are soft throughout.
2. In a large skillet over medium heat, sauté the onions, broccoli, cauliflower, and carrot in the oil for 3 to 5 minutes. Stir in the cream of mushroom soup, milk, grated cheese, and seasonings. Cook, stirring occasionally, until the cheese is completely melted and the soup is no longer lumpy (about 15 minutes).
3. Cut open the baked potatoes and top with the vegetable gravy.

Makes 4 servings.

PORTABELLA MUSHROOM PIZZA CAPS

If you're trying to reduce your intake of carbohydrates,
this is a nice alternative to pizza with crust.

4 portabella mushrooms, stems removed
1 cup Zesty Marinara Sauce (see page 145)
2 cups grated mozzarella cheese
4 tablespoons Parmesan cheese
extra-virgin olive oil

1. Set oven to broil. Place 2 small dabs of oil on a cookie sheet and rub the top and bottom of each mushroom cap in the oil, then place in the oil bottom side up and broil for 3 minutes.

2. Remove pan from oven and spread ¼ cup sauce on each mushroom cap, like a pizza. Then sprinkle ½ cup mozzarella and 1 tablespoon Parmesan on each cap. Broil for another 3 minutes.

Makes 4 servings.

Cooking Fact: Parmesan cheese, also known as Parmigiano-Reggiano, is made only in certain regions of Italy, and its designation is protected by law. Parmesan is a hard cheese made from raw cow's milk, so it is full of healthy calcium. When you get a chance, buy the real thing in the imported cheese section of your grocery store.

SOUTHWESTERN STUFFED PORTABELLA MUSHROOM CAPS

When I ate meat, I would order grilled chicken at Mexican restaurants with these types of toppings. I created this dish with those flavors in mind.

4 portabella mushrooms
⅔ cup sour cream
⅔ cup Authentic Pico de Gallo (see page 89)
⅔ cup Easy Guacamole (see page 65)
1 cup grated Monterrey Jack cheese
4 teaspoons Cholula hot sauce
canola oil

1. Set the oven to broil. Remove the stems from the mushrooms. Place 2 dabs of oil on a cookie sheet and roll both sides of the mushroom caps around in the oil.
2. Place about 1 teaspoon Cholula in the center of each upside-down mushroom cap, then tilt the cap from side to side to spread the sauce. Then place the caps bottom side up in the oil and broil for 3 minutes.
3. Make the stuffing by mixing the sour cream and pico de gallo. Put half of the mixture on each hot mushroom cap, then top each with ¼ cup Monterrey Jack cheese. Broil for another 3 minutes. Before serving, top each cap with 3 to 4 tablespoons guacamole.
4. Serve as an appetizer or over Spanish Rice (see page 117).

Makes 4 servings.

❧AVOCADO TACOS❧

I used to frequent a little taqueria in Texas that served avocado tacos for a dollar each. When I moved away, I started making the tacos for dinner at least once a week. They make a very easy, fresh meal.

4 flour tortillas
1 ripe avocado, peeled and sliced
½ lime
Authentic Pico de Gallo (see page 89)
    or Fresh Salsa (see page 75)
shredded dark green lettuce
salt to taste

Warm tortillas slightly on a griddle or frying pan. On each warmed tortilla, place a few avocado slices, then sprinkle with salt and squeeze some lime juice on top. Then top with 2 heaping spoonfuls of pico de gallo and shredded lettuce.

Makes 4 tacos.

Nutrition Tip: Dark green leafy vegetables are rich in iron, calcium, folate, vitamin A, and vitamin C. Eating these greens can promote cardiovascular health and help prevent certain types of cancers. To help the body digest dark greens properly, a small amount of fat is needed, such as extra-virgin olive oil or salad dressing.

❧EASY GUACAMOLE❧

Guacamole is a healthy snack. Try serving it on lettuce leaves or wrapping it in a tortilla.

1 ripe avocado, peeled and pitted
3 heaping spoonfuls Authentic Pico de Gallo (see page 89)
  or Fresh Salsa (see page 75)
salt to taste

Mash all ingredients together with a fork. Keep the avocado pit in the guacamole to preserve the color a little longer.

Makes 1 cup.

Nutrition Tip: Avocados contain 20 essential nutrients, including vitamin E, panthothenic acid (vitamin B_5), folate (vitamin B_9), niacin (vitamin B_3), and vitamin B_6. A diet rich in the nutrients provided by avocados has been known to reduce the risk of cardiovascular disease.

VEGGIE FAJITAS

The jalapeno flavors this dish without making it spicy. If you like spicier foods, add the whole jalapeno or perhaps two.

2 bell peppers (any color), sliced
1 onion, sliced
4 mushrooms, sliced
1 jalapeno, sliced and seeded
⅓ cup canola oil
½ teaspoon salt
¼ teaspoon pepper
¼ teaspoon chili powder
½ cup grated Monterrey Jack or cheddar cheese
12 to 16 corn or flour tortillas
Easy Guacamole (see page 65)
Fresh Salsa (see page 75)
sour cream

1. In a large frying pan over medium heat, sauté vegetables and seasonings in oil until vegetables are tender but not limp (7 to 10 minutes). When vegetables are done, sprinkle the cheese on top.
2. Serve with guacamole, salsa, sour cream, and slightly warmed tortillas,.

Makes 4 to 6 servings.

Nutrition Tip: Bell peppers are high in dietary fiber, vitamin A, vitamin C, vitamin E, vitamin B_6, and many other essential minerals. Bell peppers can assist in weight loss.

❧MEAT SUBSTITUTE❧

What I call "meat substitute" is the vegetarian version of beef crumbles usually found in the frozen food aisle of grocery stores. The brand I find most similar to beef in taste and texture is Quorn. The following recipe is a homemade beef crumble substitute. If you make this for a recipe and have leftovers, freeze them to use for future meals. Another easy homemade version of a beef crumble substitute is to crumble hard tofu and add Bragg® Liquid Aminos to taste, then cook the mixture in whatever dish you are making. For convenience, especially for those who are just beginning the journey of eating less meat, I recommend buying beef crumbles at first, to ease yourself and your family into this transition.

This meat substitute is very delicious and easy to make. It has a meaty flavor and it is full of protein. Season the meat substitute as you would season beef, or as specified by the recipe you use it in.

1 cup cooked lentils*
1 large portabella mushroom
5 to 8 white mushrooms

1. Chop the mushrooms in a food processor.
2. In a mixing bowl, stir together the lentils and chopped mushrooms.

*Freshly cooked lentils are always best. If you are using canned lentils, drain and rinse them before adding them to this recipe.

Makes 3 to 4 cups.

Nutrition Tip: Liquid aminos is a liquid protein concentrate, derived from non-genetically modified soy beans. It contains 16 amino acids and is an excellent flavor enhancer. Liquid aminos can be found at health food stores, online, and in the health food aisle in many grocery stores

STUFFED PEPPER CASSEROLE

If you have a vegetable garden, this is a great way to use up
an abundance of bell peppers.

3 bell peppers (any color)
2 cups Spanish Rice (see page 117)
1 cup Meat Substitute (see page 67)
1 cup queso fresco
3 tablespoons water
1 tablespoon canola oil
2 to 3 tablespoons chopped onion
2 garlic cloves, minced
juice from ½ lime

2 tablespoons chopped cilantro
¼ teaspoon salt

Topping:
⅓ cup diced tomatoes
½ cup shredded lettuce
½ cup sour cream
2 tablespoons Salsa Verde (see page 75)
¼ teaspoon salt

1. Preheat oven to 350ºF. Spread the Spanish Rice in a 9 x 13-inch baking dish; set aside.

2. In a small pan over medium heat, stir together the Meat Substitute, oil, water, onion, garlic, salt, and lime juice. Cook for 5 to 7 minutes or until the liquid is dissolved.

3. Cut the peppers in half, then remove the stem and seeds. Cut the queso fresco into small cubes and stir into the "meat" mixture. Spoon the mixture equally onto each pepper half, then arrange the stuffed peppers on the bed of rice.

4. In a small bowl, stir together the sour cream, Salsa Verde, and salt. Spoon equal amounts onto each stuffed pepper half.

5. Bake for 40 to 45 minutes, or until all the cheese is melted and the peppers are very tender. Sprinkle the tomatoes and lettuce on top before serving.

*Queso fresco is a soft Mexican cheese.

Makes 6 servings.

❧FAUX SLOPPY JOES❧

This dish is a real crowd pleaser, and people won't even notice it is vegetarian.

2 cups Meat Substitute (see page 67)
½ cup chopped onion
½ cup water
½ cup ketchup
1 tablespoon brown sugar
1 tablespoon white vinegar
1 tablespoon Bragg® Liquid Aminos*
½ teaspoon salt
½ teaspoon mustard
½ teaspoon chili powder
¼ teaspoon allspice
8 buns

In a large pan over medium heat, cook all ingredients until saucy but not runny (7 to 10 minutes). Then scoop desired amount onto each bun.

*Bragg® Liquid Aminos can be found at any health food store or the health food aisle at most grocery stores.

Makes 8 servings.

Nutrition Tip: Chili powder has anti-inflammatory properties and aids in reducing cardiovascular disease.

❧POTATO PANCAKES❧

These pancakes are traditionally served with a side of applesauce or sour cream. I like to eat them with both.

2 large potatoes
1 egg, beaten
⅓ cup chopped onion
2 tablespoons flour
¾ teaspoon salt
¼ teaspoon cracked pepper
canola oil
applesauce
sour cream

1. Peel the potatoes, then grate them on a cheese grater. Drain the juice from the potatoes and discard it. Mix the grated potatoes with the egg, onion, flour, salt, and pepper.
2. Pour canola oil into a frying pan until it is ¼ inch deep. Heat over medium heat, then place about ¼ cup batter in the oil and press it down with a spatula, flattening it into a pancake. Cook 3 to 4 pancakes at a time, flipping them every 3 to 4 minutes until both sides are golden brown and slightly crispy.
3. Drain pancakes on a paper towel before serving with applesauce and sour cream.

Makes 6 to 8 pancakes.

Cooking Method: Garlic Mashed Potatoes
Peel and dice 4 potatoes, then boil in water until tender. Drain the water, then mash the potatoes with 2 or 3 minced garlic cloves, ½ cup milk, 1 teaspoon salt, ½ teaspoon garlic salt, and a dash of parsley flakes. Serve hot. Makes 6 servings.

CAJUN POTATO SALAD

As a side dish, this potato salad is a delicious, healthy alternative to chips and fries.

5 medium potatoes
⅓ cup chopped onion
⅓ cup sliced celery
¼ cup relish
¼ cup canola mayonnaise
2 tablespoons mustard
½ teaspoon salt
¼ teaspoon Tony Chachere's Creole Seasoning
¼ teaspoon cracked pepper
¼ teaspoon paprika

1. Peel the potatoes, then cut into 3 or 4 large sections. Boil the potatoes until they are tender.
2. Drain the water and allow the potatoes to cool enough that you can touch them. Cut them into small chunks and place them in a large bowl. Add the rest of the ingredients to the potatoes and combine thoroughly.

Makes 8 servings.

Nutrition Tip: Consuming at least ½ cup of onions a day has been proven to reduce the risk of several types of cancers. Because they are rich in flavonoids—antioxidants with anti-inflammatory, anti-carcinogenic, and anti-allergenic properties—onions can help maintain a healthy body.

ROASTED STUFFED
MINI SWEET PEPPERS

This Latin-flavored dish is slightly sweet and very creamy.

1 dozen mini sweet peppers
¼ cup cream cheese
¼ cup grated Monterrey Jack cheese
1 teaspoon lime juice
¼ teaspoon salt
salt, to taste

1. Preheat oven to 350°F. Remove the stem and seeds from each pepper.
2. In a mixing bowl, stir together the cream cheese, Monterrey Jack cheese, lime juice, and salt. Carefully fill each pepper with the cheese mixture (try to use the same amount for each pepper).
3. Place the peppers on a lightly floured baking sheet and bake for 25 to 30 minutes, or until the cheeses are completely melted and the peppers are tender.

Makes 4 to 6 servings.

Cooking Method: Plantain Fries
Heat ¼ cup canola oil in a small frying pan over medium heat. Peel 2 plantains and cut them in half. Cut each half into 3 or 4 long, flat slices. Place the slices in a single layer in the heated oil and let cook on each side for 3 to 4 minutes. (When the plantains are done, the edges will appear slightly golden brown and crispy.) Remove slices from oil and let them dry on a paper towel. While the plantains are still hot and wet, salt them to taste. Makes 2 to 3 servings.

GARDEN FAJITAS

Who says fajitas need to contain meat? When you pack your tortilla with all of these vegetables, you won't miss the meat at all.

1 bell pepper, sliced, stem and seeds removed
1 onion, sliced
1 yellow squash, sliced
1 zucchini, sliced
4 to 6 mushrooms, sliced
¼ cup chopped cilantro
1 jalapeno, diced, stem and seeds removed
2 tablespoons lime juice
3 tablespoons olive oil
1 to 2 tablespoons water
1 teaspoon salt
½ teaspoon garlic salt
¼ teaspoon onion powder
¼ teaspoon chili powder

1. In a large skillet over medium heat, stir all ingredients together and cook, stirring occasionally, until all of the vegetables are tender.
2. Serve with sour cream, Authentic Pico de Gallo (see page 89), Easy Guacamole (see page 65), Fresh Salsa (see page 75), shredded lettuce, and warm tortillas. For side dishes, serve Vegetarian Refried Beans (see page 111) and Spanish Rice (see page 117).

Makes 4 servings.

❧STUFFED ZUCCHINI❧

If you grow your own zucchini and are looking for a new way to serve it, you'll love this recipe. It makes a great main course or side dish.

2 medium zucchinis
¼ cup ricotta cheese
¼ cup mozzarella cheese
½ teaspoon salt
½ teaspoon garlic salt
⅛ teaspoon pepper

1. Preheat oven to 450°F. Cut zucchini in half lengthwise. Bake on a cookie sheet, center side down, for 10 to 12 minutes.
2. Using a spoon, scoop out the insides of the zucchini, leaving a small layer of flesh attached to the skin. Place the scooped-out zucchini flesh in a small mixing bowl. Reduce the oven temperature to 350°F.
3. Mash the zucchini flesh, then stir in the ricotta cheese and seasonings. Fill the zucchini skins with the zucchini–cheese mixture. Sprinkle the mozzarella cheese on top. Bake for 10 to 13 minutes.

Makes 6 servings.

Cooking Tip: Fried Zucchini
Pour canola oil in the bottom of a small frying pan until it is ⅛ inch deep. Heat the oil over medium heat. Cut zucchini in lengthwise slices about ¼ inch thick. Cook for 4 to 6 minutes on each side. Dry on a paper towel, then season with salt and pepper.

❧FRESH SALSA❧

I keep my fridge stocked with fresh salsa at all times. You never know when you'll want chips and salsa or a burrito, and bottled salsa from the store just doesn't cut it.

3 tomatoes
1 red bell pepper, stem and seeds removed
½ onion
2 or 3 garlic cloves, peeled
2 jalapenos, stems and seeds removed
¼ cup cilantro
1 teaspoon sea salt, or to taste

Combine all ingredients in a blender or food processor. Purée until the desired consistency is reached.

Makes 8 servings.

❧SALSA VERDE❧

This mild, simple salsa is divine. If you are not using it in a recipe, just eat it with tortilla chips.

7 or 8 ripe tomatillos, outer skin removed
1 jalapeno, stem and seeds removed
½ cup water
¼ cup chopped onion
¼ cup cilantro
juice from 1 lemon
1 garlic clove, peeled
1 teaspoon salt

Purée all ingredients in a food processor until the desired consistency is reached.

Makes 6 cups.

CREAMED SPINACH

This is a great way to get your kids to eat spinach.

1½ cups chopped spinach (frozen is fine—just squeeze out the water)
½ cup milk
2 tablespoons sour cream
2 tablespoons cream cheese
½ teaspoon salt
¼ teaspoon onion powder
¼ teaspoon garlic powder
⅛ teaspoon cracked pepper

In a saucepan over medium heat, cook all ingredients, stirring frequently, until cream cheese is melted and the spinach is tender.

Makes 4 servings.

Nutrition Tip: Spinach is a super food loaded with vitamin A, folate, potassium, calcium, vitamin K, omega-3 fatty acids, and vitamin C. Eat it every chance you get.

SPINACH PHYLLO PIE POCKETS

If you like Greek-style spinach phyllo pie, you will love this pocket version.

1 roll frozen phyllo dough, thawed at room temperature for 2 hours
1 pound frozen chopped spinach, thawed (squeeze water out)
1 cup grated Parmesan cheese
½ cup pine nuts
2 garlic cloves, minced
¾ teaspoon salt
¼ teaspoon cracked pepper
extra-virgin olive oil
melted butter

1. Preheat oven to 350°F. In a food processor, chop the spinach, cheese, pine nuts, garlic, and seasonings together. Put the spinach mixture in a medium mixing bowl.

2. Place a little olive oil in a small bowl. Dip your fingers in the oil, then roll out a sheet of dough, lightly spreading oil across it with your fingers. Fold sheet in half. Take another sheet of dough, roll it out, fold it in half, and tuck the bottom half of the sheet in between the bottom and top halves of the first folded sheet of dough. Roll out and fold in half one more sheet of dough, then place the bottom half of the sheet between the top and bottom halves of the second sheet of dough. Repeat this entire process until you have 6 squares of dough with 6 layers each. (The layers make the crust light and flakey). Periodically dip your fingertips in olive oil to help the sheets stick together.

3. Scoop ⅓ to ½ cup spinach mixture onto the center of one square of dough. Then fold the edges of the dough over the spinach mixture, enclosing it like an envelope, and seal the edges with your fingertips. Repeat this process to make 5 more pockets.

4. Place the pockets side by side on a cookie sheet, then brush them with butter. Bake for 30 to 35 minutes.

Makes 6 servings

❧SPINACH POTATO CHEDDAR CAKES❧

Try these delicious potato patties with homemade ranch dip.

1½ cups chopped fresh spinach, packed
1 large potato, peeled and grated
2 eggs
½ cup flour
⅓ cup breadcrumbs
½ cup grated cheddar cheese
1 teaspoon sea salt
½ teaspoon onion powder
¼ teaspoon cracked pepper
2 teaspoons Cholula or Tabasco hot sauce (optional)
vegetable or canola oil

1. Fill a large skillet about ¼ inch deep with vegetable or canola oil, then heat over medium heat.
2. Chop the spinach and grate the peeled potato. Place all ingredients in a large mixing bowl and stir until well combined (you may want to use your hands).
3. Place a large scoop (about ⅓ cup) of batter in the hot oil, then press down with a spatula to flatten the batter until it is about ½ inch thick and 3 to 4 inches across. Cook the cakes in batches. Drain on paper towels.

Makes about 10 cakes.

Nutrition Tip: In recent years, potatoes have unfairly received a bad reputation. With the skin left on, they are high in vitamin C, potassium, and dietary fiber. Surprisingly, one potato even has three grams of protein. So, nourish your body with a potato every now and then—and don't feel guilty about it.

❧TWICE-BAKED POTATOES❧

A fantastic way to use leftover baked potatoes.

2 potatoes, baked
1 cup grated cheddar cheese
¼ cup sour cream
2 tablespoons milk
2 tablespoons chopped chives
½ teaspoon onion powder
½ teaspoon garlic powder
¼ teaspoon salt
¼ teaspoon pepper

1. Preheat oven to 350°F. Cut each baked potato in half lengthwise.
2. Scoop out the inside of each potato half, leaving a thin layer of potato flesh attached to the skin. Place the potato insides in a small mixing bowl and mash them with ½ cup grated cheese and the remaining ingredients. Stir until smooth.
3. Stuff the potato skins with the filling. Sprinkle the remaining cheese on top. Place the stuffed potatoes in a baking dish and bake for 15 minutes.

Makes 4 servings.

Nutrition Tip: Add a bit of flavor to your meals by stirring chives into the mix whenever you get the chance. Chives contain vitamin A and vitamin C, not a bad exchange for a little more zest in your dinner.

❧ASIAN EGGPLANT STIR-FRY❧

Serve this savory stir-fry over steamed rice or pan-fried noodles.

¼ cup soy sauce

3 tablespoons sesame oil

2 carrots, peeled and sliced

1 or 2 garlic cloves, minced

3 Japanese eggplants, cut into wedges, stems removed

1 red bell pepper, sliced

½ cup water

1 tablespoon sugar

2 teaspoons white wine vinegar

¼ teaspoon crushed chili peppers

¼ teaspoon ground ginger

¼ teaspoon salt

⅛ teaspoon paprika

⅛ teaspoon cracked pepper

1. In a large skillet over medium heat, combine the soy sauce, sesame oil, carrots, and garlic. Sauté in the oil for 3 or 4 minutes.
2. Add the remaining ingredients and continue to cook, stirring frequently, until all vegetables reach the desired tenderness.
3. If you prefer more sauce, add ¼ to ½ cup more water to the sauce.

Makes 4 to 5 servings.

Cooking Method: Grilled Eggplant

Cut an eggplant into round, ½-inch slices. (If the skin is extremely tough, you may want to cut it off.) In a mixing bowl, combine eggplant slices, 2 chopped garlic cloves, ¼ cup extra-virgin olive oil, ½ teaspoon salt, and ¼ teaspoon cracked pepper. Stir until eggplant slices are well coated. Cover bowl and let eggplant marinate for 30 minutes, then stir again. Heat grill on a low setting, then grill the eggplant slices for 5 to 7 minutes on each side. Makes 4 servings.

❧SEVEN VEGETABLE COCONUT CURRY❧

This rich and creamy curry is perfect served over steamed Jasmine rice.

1 yam, peeled and cut into chunks
½ bell pepper (any color), diced
1 cup broccoli florets
1 cup sliced mushrooms
2 cups shredded cabbage
¼ onion, sliced
2 garlic cloves, minced
3 tablespoons sesame or olive oil
1½ cups coconut milk*
¼ cup unsweetened shredded coconut
2 bay leaves
¼ teaspoon crushed red pepper
1 teaspoon sea salt
¼ teaspoon cracked pepper
1 teaspoon red curry powder

1. In a small pot, boil the yam chunks in water until they are soft but not mushy.
2. In a large skillet over medium heat, sauté the vegetables in the oil for about 5 minutes. Add the remaining ingredients, then cover and simmer for 15 to 20 minutes, stirring occasionally.

*If you are using canned coconut milk, my favorite brands are Thai Kitchen® and Whole Foods' 365™.

Makes 5 to 6 servings.

❧FAUX HAWAIIAN CHICKEN❧

I serve this yummy "chicken" over steamed rice. If you're feeding more than three people, you'll need to double the recipe.

1 cup chicken substitute*
½ cup pineapple chunks
½ cup pineapple juice
¼ cup raisins
¼ cup honey
3 tablespoons tomato paste
2 tablespoons apple cider vinegar
1 teaspoon salt
½ teaspoon mustard
¼ teaspoon garlic powder
¼ teaspoon onion powder

Preheat oven to 350°F. In an 8 x 8-inch baking dish, stir all ingredients together and bake for 20 minutes. Stir once during baking and once after. Serve over rice or noodles.

*You can find a vegetarian equivalent to chicken chunks in the frozen food aisle of the grocery store. My favorite brand is Quorn™.

Makes 3 servings.

✖BANANA WALNUT BREAD✖

This bread is so comforting and nourishing. Don't throw away those overripe bananas—make bread instead!

3 ripe bananas, peeled and mashed
2 eggs, beaten well
½ cup melted butter
½ cup raw sugar
½ cup honey
2 cups whole-wheat flour
1 teaspoon baking soda
½ teaspoon salt
1 cup chopped walnuts (optional)

1. Preheat oven to 325°F. Butter the bottom and sides of a loaf pan.
2. Mix all ingredients together, then spread batter in the pan.
3. Bake for 1 hour. Insert a toothpick in the center of the bread. If it does not come out clean, bake the bread for another 5 to 10 minutes

Makes 1 loaf.

Nutrition Tip: Eating a banana pumps you full of potassium, magnesium, and vitamin B$_6$. The fruit restores electrolytes to your system, reduces hypertension, and helps alleviate diarrhea.

ZUCCHINI SWEET BREAD

I serve this bread warm with fresh berries and whipped cream on the side.

1½ cups zucchini, grated or puréed
¾ cup sugar
⅓ cup canola oil
1 teaspoon vanilla
2 eggs
1½ cups flour
1 teaspoon baking soda
½ teaspoon sea salt
½ teaspoon cinnamon
¼ teaspoon ground cloves
¼ teaspoon baking powder
¼ cup chopped walnuts
¼ cup raisins

1. Place the oven rack on the lowest position in the oven, then preheat oven to 350°F. Lightly oil the bottom and sides of a loaf pan.
2. Using an electric mixer, mix together the first five ingredients in a large mixing bowl. Add the remaining ingredients and mix until the batter is smooth. Gently stir in the walnuts and raisins.
3. Spread the batter into the prepared loaf pan and bake on the bottom oven rack for 40 to 50 minutes, or until a toothpick inserted in the center comes out clean.

Makes 1 loaf.

❧STRAWBERRY BREAD❧

Serve this bread warm with butter or whipped cream.

1 egg, beaten well
1 cup plus 2 tablespoons flour
½ cup sugar
¼ cup canola oil
½ teaspoon vanilla
½ teaspoon baking powder
11 to 13 strawberries

1. Preheat oven to 325°F. Lightly butter a loaf pan.
2. Using a mixer, cream the sugar and oil together, then stir in the eggs and vanilla.
3. In a separate mixing bowl, combine the flour and baking powder.
4. Purée the strawberries in a blender or food processor.
5. Stir ½ cup flour mixture into the sugar mixture, then stir in half of the puréed strawberries. Continue to alternate until all ingredients are well combined.
6. Spread batter in the loaf pan and bake for 35 to 40 minutes, or until a toothpick inserted in the center of the loaf comes out clean.

Makes 1 loaf.

Nutrition Tip: One serving of strawberries provides 140% of the daily recommended amount of vitamin C. In addition, strawberries contain flavonoids, which help prevent unhealthy cholesterol from oxidizing and damaging artery walls, and ellagic acid, which helps inactivate cancer-causing chemicals in the body.

✼BLUEBERRY BANANA BREAD✼

Try this fresh from the oven with butter—the bread will melt in your mouth.

2 eggs, beaten well
1 cup sugar
3 bananas, mashed
2 cups whole-wheat flour
½ cup melted butter
1 teaspoon baking soda
½ teaspoon salt
1½ cups blueberries, fresh or frozen*

1. Preheat oven to 325°F. Lightly butter the bottom and sides of a loaf pan.
2. Combine all ingredients, except the berries, in a medium mixing bowl. Gently fold in the berries, then spread the batter in the loaf pan.
3. Bake for 60 to 75 minutes, until a toothpick inserted in the center of the loaf comes out clean.

*If using frozen blueberries, use 2 cups and set them on the counter to defrost. Drain the juice before adding the berries to the batter. By the way, the juice from the frozen berries makes a tasty, healthy drink.

Makes 1 loaf.

Nutrition Tip: Blueberries are high in vitamin A, vitamin C, and vitamin K. These tasty berries are antioxidant powerhouses and can help prevent cataracts, peptic ulcers, varicose veins, hemorrhoids, heart disease, and cancer.

BANANA MANGO SMOOTHIE

My family and I enjoy large smoothies almost every morning.
It's a great way to start the day.

1 banana
½ cup mango, cubed (fresh or frozen)
1 cup orange juice
1 cup water
2 cups ice

Place all ingredients in a blender and liquefy until the mixture reaches the desired consistency.

Makes about 4 cups (2 servings).

BLUEBERRY BLAST SMOOTHIE

This non-dairy smoothie gets its creaminess from the banana.

1 banana
1 cup blueberries (frozen or fresh)
½ cup orange juice
1 cup water
1 cup ice

Place all ingredients in a blender and liquefy until the desired consistency is reached.

Makes 2 servings.

BERRY BREEZE SMOOTHIE

With berries rich in antioxidants and a luscious color and flavor, this smoothie is a winner for parents and children alike.

2 cups mixture of blueberries, raspberries, strawberries,
    and blackberries (fresh or frozen)
1 cup tangerine juice, strawberry juice, or orange juice
1 cup water
2 cups ice

Place all ingredients in a blender and liquefy until the mixture reaches the desired consistency.

Makes about 4 cups (2 servings).

PEACH SMOOTHIE

If I had to pick a favorite smoothie, this would probably be it— it's just so good and creamy!

4 ripe peaches, peeled, pits removed
¾ cup cranberry, apple, or orange juice
½ cup water
1 cup ice

Put all ingredients in a blender and purée until the desired consistency is reached.

Makes 2 servings.

AUTHENTIC PICO DE GALLO

This pico has an authentic flavor. For added pizzazz, stir in a diced avocado.

1½ cups diced ripe tomatoes (about 3 medium tomatoes)
⅓ cup chopped onions
3 minced garlic cloves
½ jalapeno, finely chopped with the stem and seeds removed
3 tablespoons chopped cilantro
juice from ½ lime
salt, to taste
½ serrano pepper, finely chopped (optional)

Stir all ingredients together in a bowl. Add the serrano pepper for an extra-spicy flavor.

Makes 2½ cups.

VEGETABLE BARLEY PUMPKIN SOUP

The flavor in this soup will knock your sock off!

1½ cups cooked, puréed pumpkin
6 cups water
1½ cups vegetable broth
1 cup milk
2/3 cup barley
1 cup broccoli florets
1 cup cauliflower chunks
2 medium potatoes, cut into small cubes
1 carrot, peeled and sliced
1 zucchini, sliced
1 celery stalk, sliced
1 cup peas (fresh or frozen)
¼ cup chopped onion
2 garlic cloves, minced
2 tablespoons extra-virgin olive oil
1½ teaspoons sea salt
1½ teaspoons garlic salt
1 bay leaf
¼ teaspoon ground nutmeg
¼ teaspoon cracked pepper

Stir all ingredients together in a stockpot. Cover and cook over medium heat for 35 to 45 minutes, stirring occasionally. The soup is done when the potatoes and barley are soft.

BEANS, LEGUMES, AND GRAINS

❧HUMMUS❧

Hummus is an excellent party dip and a nutritious addition to a meal. Made of chickpeas, it is full of protein, iron, fiber, and, of course, flavor.

1 cup cooked chickpeas (canned is fine, drained and rinsed)
2 garlic cloves
¼ cup chopped onion
juice from 1 lemon
¼ cup tahini
1 tablespoon extra-virgin olive oil
1 tablespoon sesame oil
1 tablespoon water
¼ teaspoon salt
¼ teaspoon garlic salt
⅛ teaspoon pepper
2 dashes paprika

Purée all ingredients in a food processor. Serve as a dip for pretzels, chips, or cut vegetables such as carrots, celery, and cucumber. Hummus is also commonly served as a spread for grilled pita bread (see recipe below).

Makes 2 cups.

❧GRILLED PITA BREAD❧

1 package pita bread
extra-virgin olive oil

1. Heat griddle to 300°F, or heat a frying pan over medium heat, then lightly coat with oil.
2. Cut each pita into 6 wedges and place on the skillet or in the pan. Cook for about 1 minute each side. If using a grill, place wedges on a hot grill for about the same length of time.

Makes 60 wedges (about 10 servings).

HUMMUS AVOCADO PITA

When you can't decide whether you want to eat a salad or a sandwich, this is a perfect compromise.

4 pita breads
½ cup Hummus (see page 93)
4 cups dark green salad mix
2 avocados, sliced
½ cup diced tomatoes
⅓ cup diced onions
½ cup crumbled feta cheese
Pita Sandwich Dressing (see below)

1. In a large pan over medium heat, or a griddle heated to 300°F, warm the pita bread for 2 to 3 minutes on each side.
2. Spread 2 tablespoons hummus on each piece of pita bread, then place 1 cup salad mix on top of the hummus. Arrange avocado slices on the salad, then top with tomatoes, onions, and feta cheese. Drizzle desired amount of dressing on top.

Makes 4 servings.

PITA SANDWICH DRESSING

2 tablespoons extra-virgin olive oil
1 teaspoon balsamic vinegar
¼ teaspoon salt
⅛ teaspoon cracked pepper
dash oregano flakes

In a small bowl, mix ingredients together with a whisk or a fork.

Makes ⅓ cup.

❧SWEET POTATO SALAD❧

I love the seasonal flavor to this salad, which can easily be
served as a side dish or a meal.

2 sweet potatoes, peeled and diced
½ cup walnuts
2 celery ribs, sliced
¼ cup honey
2 tablespoons molasses
salt, to taste

Boil the sweet potato chunks until they are tender, then drain. In a serving bowl, gently stir all the ingredients together.

Makes 4 to 5 servings.

Cooking Method: Sweet Potato Wedges

Preheat oven to 375°F. Peel 2 sweet potatoes and cut into wedges. Spread wedges in a 9 x 13-inch baking dish. Cut ¼ cup butter into small cubes and sprinkle over the wedges, then top with ¼ cup brown sugar. Bake for 40 to 45 minutes or until the potatoes are completely tender, stirring 2 to 3 times while baking. Remove from oven and season with salt to taste. Makes 4 to 5 servings.

❧CORN MUFFINS❧

These muffins are sweetened with agave nectar instead of honey or sugar.
The thick batter makes very moist muffins.

1 cup whole-wheat or all-purpose flour
1 cup cornmeal
2 teaspoons baking powder
½ teaspoon sea salt
3 tablespoons agave nectar
¾ cup milk
¼ cup canola oil
1 egg, beaten well

1. Preheat oven to 350°F. Line a muffin pan with paper liners.
2. In a mixing bowl, whisk together the dry ingredients, then add the remaining ingredients. Mix thoroughly but do not beat.
3. Fill each muffin cup about ¾ full with batter. Bake muffins for 20 to 25 minutes, or until a toothpick inserted in the center comes out clean.
4. To make cornbread, spread the batter in an 8 x 8-inch pan and bake at 375°F for 20 to 25 minutes.

Makes 24 servings.

Cooking Method: Black-eyed Peas
In a slow cooker, combine 1 pound dried black-eyed peas, 4 cups water, 1½ cups vegetable broth, ¼ cup chopped onion, 1½ teaspoons salt, 1½ teaspoons garlic salt, ½ teaspoon onion powder, ½ teaspoon garlic powder, and ½ teaspoon parsley flakes. Cover and cook on high heat for 2 to 2½ hours. Makes 8 to 10 servings. (In the South, black-eyed peas are traditionally served with cornbread.)

CORN CHOWDER

This creamy soup is perfect for corn lovers.

2 cans cream-style corn
1 cup milk
1 potato, peeled and diced
1 carrot, sliced
3 cups water
¼ cup chopped onion
2 teaspoons butter
1 teaspoon dried thyme
¾ teaspoon salt
⅛ teaspoon cracked pepper

In a stockpot, cook the butter, onions, carrot, and potato for 5 to 6 minutes. Add the rest of the ingredients and cook until the potatoes are soft, about 20 to 30 minutes.

Makes 4 servings.

Cooking Method: Corn Off the Cob

In a large pot, boil ears of corn in plenty of water for 15 minutes. When corn reaches the desired tenderness, remove it from the water. On a cutting board, stand an ear of corn up and stick a fork in the top to hold it still. While keeping one hand on the fork for stability, use a sharp, serrated knife to cut the corn off the cob. Repeat the process with each ear of corn, then place the corn in a serving bowl with some butter (about 2 tablespoons for 6 ears of corn), and stir together until the butter is melted. Season with salt and pepper, to taste.

CREAMY WHITE-BEAN SOUP

This is a hearty bean-and-vegetable soup full of protein and wholesome flavor

6 cups water
1½ cups vegetable broth
1 pound small white dried beans
1 carrot, peeled and sliced
1 celery stalk, sliced
1 cup milk
1 can cream of onion soup*
¼ cup chopped onion
¼ cup chopped cilantro
½ cup frozen green peas
2 tablespoons extra-virgin olive oil
1 teaspoon salt
¼ teaspoon cracked pepper
1 cup shredded mozzarella cheese

1. Rinse the dried beans and remove any rocks and other debris.
2. In a stockpot over medium-high heat, stir together the water, vegetable broth, and beans. Bring to a boil, then add the remaining ingredients except the cheese. Cover the pot and reduce heat to medium. Cook for 2½ to 3 hours, stirring occasionally.
3. When the soup is done, gently stir in the cheese until it melts and there are no clumps.

*Cream of mushroom soup may be substituted.

Makes 8 to 10 servings.

LENTIL SOUP

This lentil soup is very thick and filling, so you won't need to serve it with anything except perhaps crackers.

2 cups dried lentils
7 cups water
1 can vegetable broth
2 carrots, peeled and sliced
¼ cup chopped onion
3 or 4 garlic cloves, minced
1 teaspoon salt
1 teaspoon garlic salt
½ teaspoon oregano flakes
¼ teaspoon ground cumin
¼ teaspoon cracked pepper

Combine all ingredients in a stockpot. Cover and cook over medium-high heat for 1 hour, stirring occasionally.

Makes 6 to 8 servings.

Nutrition Tip: Lentils are a great source of protein, fiber, and iron. If you're just starting to eat less meat, regularly adding lentils to your diet will help ease the transition.

SPLIT-PEA AND BARLEY SOUP

Split-pea soup has been a favorite of mine since I was a child, when my mother would make it on occasion. I serve it with fresh, warm rolls and butter.

1 pound dried split peas, rinsed
½ cup barley, uncooked
5 cups water
2 cans vegetable broth
½ cup chopped onions
1 carrot, peeled and sliced
¼ cup chopped cilantro
1 teaspoon salt
1 teaspoon garlic salt
½ teaspoon cracked pepper
½ teaspoon Tony Chachere's Creole Seasoning (optional)

Combine all ingredients in a stockpot, then cover and cook for 1½ hours. Stir soup and mash the peas occasionally.

Makes 6 to 8 servings.

Nutrition Tip: Barley is high in iron, folic acid, selenium, and omega-6 fatty acids. One-half cup cooked barley contains 4 grams of protein.

GARDEN GUMBO

Gumbo can be an acquired taste for people unaccustomed to such flavor combinations. However if you like Cajun-style gumbo, you will enjoy this version of it.

½ cup plus 3 tablespoons canola oil
½ cup plus 1 tablespoon flour
4 cups water
3 cans vegetable broth
3 collard-green leaves, shredded
1 cup sliced okra
1 plantain, sliced
½ cup sliced grape tomatoes
2 celery stalks, sliced
2 garlic cloves, minced
1 bell pepper, diced
½ cup chopped onion
½ cup chopped cilantro
1 tablespoon dried sage
1 teaspoon salt
½ teaspoon cracked pepper
1 to 2 tablespoons Tabasco sauce
steamed rice

1. In a stockpot, heat oil over medium heat, then stir in flour. Continue stirring and cooking until the mixture turns dark brown, about 15 minutes.
2. In a separate pan, heat 3 tablespoons oil. Sauté the vegetables until tender (7 to 10 minutes).
3. Add seasonings, vegetables, water, and broth to flour mixture. Simmer uncovered for 30 minutes
4. Serve over steamed rice.

Makes 10 to 12 servings.

❧VEGETARIAN CHILI❧

Although this chili is delicious by itself, I usually serve it over baked potatoes or bowls of Frito chips, topped with grated cheddar cheese.

1 large onion, diced
2 poblano peppers, diced, stems and seeds removed
1 large red bell pepper, diced, stem and seeds removed
6 garlic cloves, minced
2 tablespoons extra-virgin olive oil
28-ounce can crushed tomatoes (do not drain)
12-ounce can tomato paste
2 tablespoons chili powder
2 tablespoons Bragg® Liquid Aminos*
1 tablespoon ground cumin
2 teaspoons dried thyme
2 teaspoons chopped fresh cilantro
½ teaspoon salt
½ teaspoon pepper
1 can kidney beans, drained and rinsed
1 can chickpeas, drained and rinsed
1 can hominy, drained and rinsed

In a stockpot, sauté onion, peppers, carrots, and garlic in oil for 15 minutes or until tender. Stir in remaining ingredients and bring to a boil. Reduce heat and simmer 30 minutes.

*Bragg® Liquid Aminos can be found at any health food store, or in the health food aisle of a grocery store.

Makes 12 servings.

> Nutrition Tip: Chickpeas (garbanzo beans) are very high in protein, calcium, folate, and fiber.

❧BLACK BEAN CHILI❧

This is my children's favorite food on a cold day. I usually serve it over a bowl of corn chips and topped with grated cheddar cheese.

1 pound dried black beans
4 cups water
1 can vegetable broth
two 12-ounce cans tomato paste
2 carrots, peeled and sliced
1 bell pepper, diced
⅓ cup chopped onion
¼ cup chopped cilantro
2 or 3 garlic cloves, minced
2 tablespoons Bragg® Liquid Aminos*
1 tablespoon extra-virgin olive oil
2 teaspoons chili powder
1½ teaspoons salt
1 teaspoon garlic salt
½ teaspoon cracked pepper

Combine all ingredients in a slow cooker and cook on high for 4½ to 5 hours. Stir occasionally.

*Bragg® Liquid Aminos can be found at any health food store or the health food aisle at most grocery stores.

Makes 8 to 10 servings.

Nutrition Tip: Black beans are packed with protein, iron, folate, and calcium, as well as fiber and healthy carbohydrates.

WHITE BEAN CHILI

I serve this over bowls of Fritos® chips and grated cheese.

3 cups cooked white beans (if using canned, drain and rinse them)
15-ounce can Rotel® diced tomatoes with green chilies
2 bell peppers (any color), diced
1 onion, chopped
3 tablespoons extra-virgin olive oil
1 celery rib, sliced
1 carrot, sliced
3 tablespoons Bragg® Liquid Aminos*
1 teaspoon sea salt
1 teaspoon garlic salt
½ teaspoon chili powder
¼ teaspoon pepper
two 16-ounce cartons V8® golden butternut squash soup

1. In a stockpot over medium heat, sauté the vegetables and seasonings in the oil and Bragg® Liquid Aminos for about 10 minutes.
2. Stir in the remaining ingredients and cook for about 15 minutes, or until all of the flavors are well combined and the vegetables are soft.

*Bragg® Liquid Aminos can be found at any health food store or the health food aisle at most grocery stores.

Makes 8 servings.

WHITE BEAN AND KALE SOUP

My children fell in love with kale when I invented this soup. It is delicious served with freshly baked bread.

2 cups vegetable broth
8 cups water
1½ cups cream
1 pound dried great northern beans
2 cups chopped kale
⅓ cup chopped onion
3 garlic cloves, minced
2 carrots, sliced
juice from 1 naval orange
1 bay leaf
2½ teaspoons salt
½ teaspoon ground cumin
¼ teaspoon crushed red pepper
¼ teaspoon cracked pepper

1. Rinse the beans and discard any debris.
2. In a stockpot over medium-high heat, bring the liquid and beans to a boil, then add the seasonings. Cover the soup and let boil for an hour.
3. Add the remaining ingredients, cover again, and cook for another hour. The soup is ready when the beans are soft.

Makes 6 to 8 servings.

CUBAN BLACK BEANS

These beans are great over Savory Rice (see page 116) or Spanish Rice (see page 117). I serve diced tomatoes, diced avocados, shredded lettuce, and grated cheese as toppings for the beans.

2 cups dried black beans
10 cups water
¼ cup diced onion
2 tablespoons extra-virgin olive oil
2 tablespoons chopped cilantro
2 bay leaves
2 garlic cloves, minced
1 teaspoon oregano flakes
1 teaspoon cumin seeds
½ teaspoon salt
½ teaspoon cracked pepper
¼ teaspoon garlic salt

1. Rinse the beans and remove any rocks and other debris.
2. Place all ingredients in a stockpot. Bring to a boil, then cover and cook over medium heat, stirring occasionally, for 2½ to 3 hours or until beans are soft.

Makes 10 to 12 servings.

RED BEANS AND RICE

*This Southern staple is traditionally served with Corn Muffins (see page 95).
My family enjoys eating these beans and rice in burritos
with grated cheese and Salsa Verde (see page 75).*

1 pound dried kidney beans, soaked overnight
5 cups water
1 can vegetable broth
1 green bell pepper, diced
¼ onion, diced
2½ teaspoons salt
1½ teaspoon Cholula hot sauce
1 teaspoon ground cumin
¼ teaspoon cracked pepper
½ teaspoon chili powder
2 cups rice

1. Place all ingredients, except the rice, in a slow cooker. Stir well, cover, and cook on high for 4½ hours.
2. Stir in the rice and let cook another 30 minutes. If the liquid is cooked out but the rice is not yet tender, add 1 to 2 cups more water, then cover and cook until water is cooked out and the rice is tender.

Makes 6 to 8 servings.

SOUTHWESTERN QUINOA AND BLACK-BEAN SALAD

Quinoa has a fluffy texture and a slightly nutty taste. It is an excellent source of vegan protein and contains many other important nutrients.

¾ cup quinoa
1 cup water
½ cup cooked black beans (if using canned, drain and rinse them)
½ cup corn (frozen is fine)
¼ cup diced tomatoes
¼ cup chopped onion
2 tablespoons chopped fresh cilantro
1 teaspoon Cholula hot sauce
1 teaspoon extra-virgin olive oil
1 teaspoon lime juice
1 teaspoon sea salt
1 avocado, sliced

1. Soak the quinoa in a bowl of water for 15 minutes to an hour.
2. Place the soaked quinoa in a small pot with the water, black beans, and corn. Cover and cook until the quinoa is soft and the water is cooked out, about 15 minutes.
3. Scoop the cooked quinoa mixture into a mixing bowl, then gently stir in the tomatoes, onions, Cholula sauce, olive oil, lime juice, and salt.
4. Drizzle Cholula on top and serve with avocado slices.

Makes 2 to 3 servings.

BLACK BEAN WRAPS

Cuban Black Beans (see page 105) are excellent in these wraps.

1 bell pepper, sliced
½ onion, sliced
2 tablespoons extra-virgin olive oil
¼ teaspoon Tony Chachere's Creole Seasoning
6 tortillas
½ cup grated cheddar cheese
1½ cups black beans (if using canned, drain and rinse them)
½ cup guacamole (see page 65)
1 cup shredded lettuce

1. In a small pan, sauté the peppers and onions in the oil and Creole seasoning.
2. Warm a tortilla on a griddle or large frying pan, then sprinkle with a little cheese. Once cheese melts, remove the tortilla from the heat. Repeat with remaining tortillas.
3. Place about ¼ cup beans on each tortilla, then add a large spoonful of peppers and onions. Top with 2 to 3 tablespoons guacamole and a small handful of lettuce. Then roll up the tortilla and enjoy.

Makes 6 servings.

Nutrition Tip: To reduce canned beans' sodium content by about 40%, drain and rinse the beans in a colander before adding them to a recipe.

❧ WESTERN PINTO BEANS ❧

A common misconception is that pinto beans must be cooked with ham hocks. Actually, beans have just as much flavor when cooked with simple vegetables and spices.

2 cups dried pinto beans
12 cups water
3 cups vegetable broth
½ cup chopped onion
¼ cup chopped cilantro
juice from 1 lime
4 garlic cloves, minced
2 tablespoons Cholula hot sauce
2 teaspoons thyme
2 teaspoons salt
½ teaspoon cracked pepper

1. Rinse the beans and remove any debris. In a stockpot, combine all ingredients, cover, and cook on medium-high heat, stirring occasionally, for 3 hours or until beans are tender.
2. Serve these beans in burritos, in bean bowls (with grated cheese, avocado slices, diced tomatoes, and shredded lettuce), or over Savory Rice (see page 116) or Spanish Rice (see page 117). On occasion, I put some pinto beans in casseroles and pastas to add protein and bulk to the meal.

Makes 8 servings.

Nutrition Tip: Pinto beans are full of protein, iron, fiber, folate, and potassium, plus omega-3 and omega-6 fatty acids.

BAKED BEANS

The sauce for these beans is divine. If you're serving them as a side dish and you're feeding more than five people, double the recipe.

3 cups cooked white beans
1 cup bean broth*
⅓ cup brown sugar
⅓ cup molasses
¼ cup tomato paste
1½ teaspoons salt
1 teaspoon cornstarch
½ teaspoon mustard
½ teaspoon onion powder
½ teaspoon paprika
½ teaspoon garlic powder

Preheat oven to 400°F. Stir all ingredients together in a 2-quart or 8 x 8-inch baking dish. Bake for 30 minutes, stirring once during baking.

*Rather than using canned beans, I prefer to cook the beans and use the bean broth from the pot. However, if you are using canned beans, just drain the beans and reserve the liquid, then rinse the beans. You may need to add water to the liquid to equal 1 cup of bean broth.

Makes 5 servings.

❧ VEGETARIAN REFRIED BEANS ❧

Freshly cooked beans always taste best, but if you're pressed for time, canned beans work just fine in this recipe.

2 cups cooked pinto beans (see Western Pinto Beans, page 109)
¼ cup canola oil
½ teaspoon salt
¼ teaspoon chili powder
¼ teaspoon onion powder
¼ teaspoon garlic powder

In a skillet over medium heat, mash beans with a large wooden spoon, then stir in remaining ingredients. Stir and cook until beans are heated throughout.

Makes 2 cups.

Cooking Method: Roasted and Salted Nuts

Heat oven to 400°F. In a medium bowl, cover 2 cups raw nuts with water for about 10 seconds. Drain the water, then sprinkle 1 teaspoon salt over the nuts and stir it well. Spread the nuts on a cookie sheet. Bake for 4 minutes, stir, and then bake for 2 more minutes. Makes 4 servings.

FRIED BEAN AND CHEESE BURRITOS

With crispy-fried outsides and soft centers, these burritos are tantalizing.

1½ cups Vegetarian Refried Beans (see page 111)
1 cup grated cheddar cheese
4-ounce can green chilies (optional)
6 to 8 flour tortillas
canola oil
Fresh Salsa (see page 75)

1. Pour canola oil in a small frying pan until it is about ½ inch deep. Heat the oil over medium heat.
2. Place 2 to 3 large spoonfuls of refried beans down the center of a tortilla, then add desired amount of cheese and 1 to 2 teaspoons green chilies. Fold in the sides and ends of the tortilla like an envelope. Repeat the process with each tortilla.
3. Fry the burritos on each side for 4 to 6 minutes, or until they are golden brown and slightly crispy. Drain on paper towels.

Makes 6 to 8 servings.

❧TOSTADAS❧

Richard Swain, my children's grandpa from Texas, is the Tostada King in our family, and we have him to thank for these tasty creations.

1 package tostada shells
3 cups grated cheddar cheese
1 cup Vegetarian Refried Beans (see page 111)
bottled sliced jalapeños
Authentic Pico de Gallo (see page 89)
shredded lettuce

Preheat oven to 350°F. Spread tostadas on cookie sheets and bake for 3 to 4 minutes. Remove from oven and let cool for a few minutes.

Cheese Tostadas:
Cover each tostada with about ¼ cup cheese, then top with 3 to 5 jalapeno slices. Bake until cheese is completely melted (5 to 7 minutes).

Bean and Cheese Tostadas:
Spread a large spoonful of beans on each tostada and bake for 3 to 5 minutes. Remove from oven and sprinkle each tostada with about ⅛ cup cheese. Top with pico de gallo and lettuce.

Makes 10 servings.

❧MEXICAN CORNBREAD
CASSEROLE❧

Any cornbread batter will do fine for this meal. If you use a packaged mix, I recommend Jiffy® brand.

1½ cups Meat Substitute (see page 67)
cornbread batter (see Corn Muffins, page 95)
1 cup grated cheddar cheese
¾ cup frozen corn, defrosted
4-ounce can green chilies
2 tablespoons chopped onions
2 tablespoons canola oil
2 tablespoons water
¼ teaspoon salt
¼ teaspoon chili powder
¼ teaspoon garlic salt
Easy Guacamole (see page 65)
Fresh Salsa (see page 75)

1. Preheat oven to 400°F. Butter an 8 x 8-inch baking dish.
2. In a small frying pan over medium heat, cook the Meat Substitute, onions, oil, water, and spices for 3 to 5 minutes, stirring frequently.
3. Mix the cornbread batter according to package instructions. Mix in the cheese, corn, chilies, and "meat" mixture.
4. Spread the batter into the baking dish. Bake until a toothpick inserted in the center comes out clean, about 20 to 25 minutes.
5. Serve with salsa and/or guacamole on the side.

Makes 6 servings.

❧NACHOS❧

Nachos are a party favorite for young and old alike. If serving this dish to more than three people, just double the recipe.

1 cup Meat Substitute (see page 67)
⅓ cup black beans (canned are fine, just drain and rinse them)
¼ cup water
¼ cup picante sauce or salsa
1½ cups grated cheddar cheese
2 to 3 large handfuls tortilla chips
¼ teaspoon salt
⅛ teaspoon chili powder
sour cream
Authentic Pico de Gallo (see page 89)
Easy Guacamole (see page 65)
1 cup shredded lettuce

1. Preheat oven to 350°F. In a small frying pan, mix the Meat Substitute, beans, water, picante sauce or salsa, salt, and chili powder. Cook over medium heat until water is absorbed (6 to 8 minutes).
2. Spread the chips on a cookie sheet. Sprinkle the "meat" mixture over the chips, then the cheese. Bake for 7 to 10 minutes, until all the cheese is melted.
3. Remove pan from oven. Sprinkle nachos with pico de gallo and shredded lettuce. Serve with sour cream and guacamole on the side.

Makes 3 servings.

SAVORY RICE

This rice goes well with just about any bean dish.

1½ cups brown rice or long-grain white rice
3¼ cups water
2 garlic cloves, minced
2 tablespoons extra-virgin olive oil
½ teaspoon salt
¼ teaspoon cracked pepper

Place all ingredients in a medium saucepan. Cover pan and cook over medium heat for 20 to 30 minutes, or until the rice is soft.

Makes 4 to 5 servings.

Cooking Method: White and Green Beans

Remove the ends from 1 pound of raw green beans. Discard the ends. Wash the beans and cut them into 1-inch segments. Steam over medium heat for 5 minutes. Gently stir in ½ cup water, 1½ cups cooked great northern beans (if using canned, drain and rinse them), 1 tablespoon butter, 1 tablespoon lime juice, 2 teaspoons Dijon mustard, ¼ teaspoon salt, and ¼ teaspoon cracked pepper. Cook for another 5 minutes. Makes 4 to 5 servings. To make a meal of this dish, serve it over Savory Rice (see page 116).

SPANISH RICE

This rice is a perfect companion to any Latin dish.

¼ cup chopped onion
1 garlic clove
1 tomato
¼ cup canola oil
1½ cups brown rice or long-grain white rice
1 can vegetable broth
½ cup frozen green peas
1 carrot, peeled and sliced
2½ cups water
1 teaspoon salt

1. Purée onion, garlic, and tomato in a blender or food processor.
2. In a large frying pan over medium heat, combine the puréed mixture with the oil and rice. Cook for 5 to 7 minutes, stirring frequently.
3. Add the remaining ingredients, cover, and cook until water is steamed out and rice is tender (about 30 minutes).

Makes 8 servings.

Nutrition Tip: Green peas are high in vitamin C and vitamin K, as well as a plethora of other vitamins and minerals. In addition, a 3-ounce serving of raw green peas contains 5 grams of protein. The nutrients in peas can help improve the health of your bones and your heart.

VEGETABLE FRIED RICE

This dish is a meal all by itself. It also goes well with Chinese Cashew Vegetable Stir-Fry (see page 50) and Cream Cheese Wontons (see page 34).

2 cups steamed rice
2 eggs, beaten slightly
2 mushrooms, sliced
1 celery stalk, sliced
1 carrot, peeled and sliced
½ cup green peas (frozen are okay)
2 Chinese cabbage leaves, shredded
4 tablespoons canola oil, divided
3 tablespoons soy sauce
2 tablespoons chopped red onion
1 dash cracked pepper

1. In a large skillet over medium heat, sauté mushrooms, celery, and carrots in 1 tablespoon of oil for 2 to 3 minutes.
2. Add 2 tablespoons oil, along with rice, peas, cabbage, and onion. Cook and stir for 5 to 7 minutes.
3. Push mixture to the edges of the pan to create a well. In the well, place 1 tablespoon oil and then the eggs. Cook eggs, stirring frequently, until they are thickened but still a little soft. Gradually stir the eggs, soy sauce, and pepper into the rice mixture.

❧BROCCOLI, CHEESE, AND RICE CASSEROLE❧

*Kids of all ages enjoy the taste of broccoli and cheese mixed with rice.
To pack this dish with even more nutrition, use wild rice.*

1 cup brown or long-grain white rice

2 cups water

1½ cups grated cheddar cheese, divided

2 cups chopped broccoli

¼ cup chopped onion

2 tablespoons butter

1 teaspoon flour

¾ teaspoon salt

¼ teaspoon mustard

¼ teaspoon pepper

½ cup milk

1. Cook the rice in the water until the water is cooked out and the rice is tender.
2. Preheat oven to 350°F. In a saucepan, melt the butter, then add the flour, salt, mustard, and pepper. Stir in the milk. Once the mixture is smooth, stir in the broccoli and cook for 5 minutes.
3. In a 9 x 13-inch baking dish, mix together the rice, the broccoli mixture, and 1 cup of cheese. Spread the mixture evenly in the dish. Sprinkle the remaining cheese on top. Bake for about 30 minutes.

Makes 6 to 8 servings.

Nutrition Tip: Because it contains high levels of vitamins A and C—both antioxidants—Chinese cabbage has anti-inflammatory properties. It also contains a significant amount of calcium. This cabbage tastes great in salads, in stir-fries, or simply steamed and served with rice and soy sauce.

SPINACH PARMESAN RISOTTO

*This dish tastes great with Roma tomatoes and
extra Parmesan cheese sprinkled on top.*

2 tablespoons extra-virgin olive oil
2 garlic cloves, minced
1 cup fresh spinach, packed
1 cup rice
1¼ cups water
1 can vegetable broth
½ cup grated Parmesan cheese
½ teaspoon salt
¼ teaspoon garlic salt
¼ teaspoon cracked pepper

1. In a large skillet over medium heat, cook the garlic in the oil for 1 minute.
2. Add the spinach and spices, cooking and stirring until the spinach is wilted.
3. Stir in the rice, then add the remaining ingredients. Cover and cook for 25 to 30 minutes, stirring occasionally, until rice is tender. If the liquid cooks out before the rice is completely softened, add a little more water, then cover and cook a bit longer.

Makes 4 servings.

MUSHROOM RISOTTO

This risotto has a very sophisticated flavor.

1 cup warm water
¼ cup dried porcini mushrooms, packed
10 ounces white mushrooms, sliced (about 2½ cups)
1 portabella mushroom, stem removed, cut into cubes
2 garlic cloves
¼ cup extra-virgin olive oil
1½ teaspoons salt
1½ teaspoons garlic salt
¼ teaspoon pepper
2 cups rice
1 can vegetable broth
2½ cups water
1 cup Parmesan cheese (optional)

1. In a small bowl, soak the porcini mushrooms in 1 cup of warm water for 30 minutes. Drain the mushrooms, reserving the water.
2. In a large skillet over medium-high heat, sauté the white mushrooms, portabella mushroom, and garlic in the olive oil for 10 to 12 minutes.
3. Add the remaining ingredients, including the porcini mushrooms and soaking water, to the skillet. Cover and cook for 30 to 40 minutes, stirring occasionally. If rice is not tender enough, add ½ cup water and cook until rice is tender and liquid is cooked out.

Makes 4 to 5 servings.

FAUX CHICKEN AND RICE CAKES

These cakes resemble crab cakes and are quite appetizing. If you'd like to serve them with a sauce, try the Mozzarella Sauce (see page 157).

1 cup chicken substitute*
1 cup steamed rice
1 egg, beaten well
½ cup carrots
½ cup green peas
2 tablespoons chopped onion
2 tablespoons flour
½ teaspoon salt
½ teaspoon garlic salt
¼ teaspoon cracked pepper
canola oil

1. Put the chicken substitute in the fridge (or on the counter if you're pressed for time) to thaw until soft. Then place the chicken substitute, rice, carrots, and onion in a food processor and purée or chop into very small chunks.
2. Place a thin layer of canola oil in a frying pan and warm the oil over medium heat.
3. In a medium mixing bowl, mash together the puréed mixture, egg, peas, flour, and seasonings. Using your hands, form round cakes about ½ inch thick and 3 inches wide.
4. Place the cakes in the heated oil side by side (cook 3 to 5 at a time). While the cakes are cooking, gently press them with a spatula to allow the cakes to fry evenly in the center. Fry the cakes for about 10 minutes on each side. They will be slightly crispy and golden brown. Remove the cakes from the oil and let dry on a paper towel before serving.

*You can find an equivalent vegetarian to chicken chunks in the frozen food aisle of most grocery stores. My favorite brand is Quorn.

Makes 4 servings.

❧ VEGGIE BURGERS ❧

These are so much tastier than ground-beef patties and store-bought frozen vegetarian patties. Serve the patties as you would a hamburger patty—on a bun with all your favorite fixings. I like my veggie burger with melted pepper Jack cheese plus avocado slices, tomatoes, onions, and dark green lettuce.

1 can black beans, rinsed and drained
1 portabella mushroom
1 cup water
½ cup dried brown rice
1 cup whole-wheat flour
½ cup rolled oats
½ cup grated mozzarella or Monterrey Jack cheese
1½ teaspoons sea salt
1½ teaspoons garlic powder
canola oil or extra-virgin olive oil

1. Steam rice according to package instructions. Heat a griddle to 300°F. (Do not grill these patties—their shape won't hold).
2. Purée beans, mushroom, and water in a food processor until smooth but still slightly chunky. Place the bean mixture in a mixing bowl, then add the remaining ingredients and stir until they are well combined.
3. Lightly coat the griddle or frying pan with oil. With your hands, form one thick, round patty at a time. (The batter will be slightly runny but will firm up when cooking.)
4. Place patties on the oiled pan or griddle, then press the centers down with a spatula to make the patties about ½ inch thick. Cook patties on each side for 4 to 6 minutes.

If you want to freeze patties for future use, just form each patty on a parchment-paper-lined cookie sheet, then put the cookie sheet in the freezer. Once patties are frozen, remove them from the cookie sheet, place them in a ziptop freezer bag, and put the bag in the freezer. Cook frozen patties for an additional 2 to 4 minutes.

Makes 10 to 12 servings.

VEGGIE CORN DOGS

*These are always a treat at my house, and guests have no idea
the corn dogs are vegetarian.*

1 package vegetarian hot dogs
wooden skewers
½ cup whole-wheat flour
⅓ cup cornmeal
1 egg, beaten well
½ cup water
¼ cup oil
2 tablespoons milk
1 teaspoon honey
½ teaspoon salt
¼ teaspoon baking soda

1. Preheat oven to 400°F. Lightly oil a cookie sheet.
2. With a wire whisk, mix flour, cornmeal, egg, water, oil, milk, honey, salt, and baking soda until the mixture is no longer lumpy.
3. Skewer each hot dog by placing the sharp end of a skewer into the end of the hot dog and driving the skewer through the long way, stopping about an inch from the end of the hot dog.
4. Dip and roll hot dogs in the batter until they are completely covered. Place dipped hot dogs side by side on the cookie sheet, leaving about 2 inches of space between them.
5. Bake for 7 to 10 minutes or until batter is completely cooked.

If you prefer mini corn dogs to large corn dogs on a stick, simply cut each vegetarian hot dog into thirds before dipping it in the batter. The baking time does not change.

Makes 4 servings.

QUINOA JAMBALAYA

A pseudo grain that is actually a seed, quinoa is full of vegan protein and many other nutrients. Quinoa can be substituted in any recipe calling for rice or couscous.

1½ cups cooked beans (I use kidney
    beans, but any variety would be fine)
1 cup sausage substitute crumbles*
2 tablespoons extra-virgin olive oil
¼ cup chopped onion
¼ cup chopped bell pepper
¼ cup chopped celery
2 garlic cloves, minced
½ cup diced tomatoes
2 bay leaves
1 tablespoon Bragg® Liquid Aminos

1 to 2 teaspoons Tabasco sauce
¾ cup quinoa
1½ cups vegetable broth
1½ cups water
1 teaspoon sea salt
1 teaspoon paprika
½ teaspoon garlic powder
½ teaspoon oregano flakes
½ teaspoon cayenne pepper
¼ teaspoon black pepper

In a large skillet, sauté the vegetables in the oil for a few minutes, then stir in the dry quinoa until it is coated in oil. Stir in the remaining ingredients and cover the skillet. Let steam 20 to 30 minutes or until the quinoa is soft, stirring occasionally.

*Sausage substitute is available in the freezer section of most grocery stores with the rest of the Meat Substitutes. Also, I have discovered a sausage substitute that is refrigerated, not frozen. It is usually found in the refrigerated section of the produce aisle. It tastes great, and the soy in it is not genetically modified. It is called Gimme Lean®. If you choose to use it instead of frozen sausage substitute, you'll need to brown it in a bit of oil first, then remove it from the skillet and continue with the recipe as described, stirring in the browned, crumbled sausage substitute just after the quinoa.

Makes 8 to 10 servings.

❧GRANOLA❧

This granola is excellent with berries and yogurt or milk.

1½ cups rolled oats
¼ cup raisins
⅓ cup pecan or almond pieces
2 tablespoons brown sugar
1½ tablespoons honey
1 tablespoon wheat germ
1 tablespoon flaxseed
1½ teaspoons vanilla

1. Preheat oven to 350°F. Stir all ingredients together in a mixing bowl.
2. Spread mixture on a cookie sheet. Bake for 4 minutes, then stir and bake an additional 2 to 4 minutes.
3. Remove from heat and spread granola on a plate to cool.

Makes 2½ cups.

Nutrition Tip: Oats contain healthy doses of folate, protein, potassium, and Omega-6 fatty acids.

❧CHEWY GRANOLA BARS❧

These granola bars are so chewy and delicious, you'll never want to eat store-bought granola bars again.

2 cups old-fashioned oats
1 cup flour
¾ cup brown sugar
½ cup wheat germ
1 tablespoon golden flaxseed
¾ teaspoon cinnamon
¾ teaspoon salt
⅓ cup honey
½ cup canola oil
3 tablespoons maple syrup
1 egg, beaten well
⅓ cup mini chocolate chips, raisins, chopped pecans, or chopped almonds

1. Preheat oven to 350°F. Butter a 9 x 13-inch cake pan.
2. In a large mixing bowl, stir together oats, flour, brown sugar, wheat germ, cinnamon, flaxseed, and salt. Make a well in the center, then place the rest of the ingredients in the well and mix thoroughly with your hands (the mixture will be very sticky).
3. Using your hands, spread the mixture evenly into the cake pan. Bake for 25 minutes or until the edges are golden brown. Remove pan from oven and let sit for 10 to 15 minutes. Cut into 3-inch squares while still warm.

Makes 16 to 20 bars.

Nutrition Tip: Raw almonds have more protein than any other nut and also contain significant amounts of calcium, folate, fiber, vitamin E, and omega-6 fatty acids.

PEANUT BUTTER
GRANOLA BARS

*I make these energy-charging granola bars for hikes or camping trips.
They make a perfect on-the-go snack.*

2 cups rolled oats
¾ cup brown sugar
½ cup wheat germ
1 tablespoon flaxseed
¾ teaspoon salt
½ cup crunchy peanut butter
¼ cup honey
¼ cup canola oil
1 egg, beaten well
2 tablespoons maple syrup*

1. Preheat oven to 350°F. Lightly butter the inside of a 9 x 13-inch baking dish.
2. In a large mixing bowl, combine the oats, brown sugar, wheat germ, flaxseed, and salt. Make a well in the center of the mixture, then place the remaining ingredients in the well. With your hands, mix all ingredients together; the mixture will be very sticky. Spread evenly in the baking dish.
3. Bake for 20 minutes or until the edges are a slightly darker golden brown. Remove from oven and cool for 10 to 15 minutes, then cut into bars. (It is much easier to cut the bars while they are still warm.)

*Be sure to use 100% maple syrup.

Makes 16 to 20 bars.

Nutrition Tip: The peanut, a legume, is high in protein, calcium, folate, and many other important nutrients.

❧OATMEAL PANCAKES❧

I've been making oatmeal pancakes since I was a teenager.
It's a healthier way to eat fluffy, delicious pancakes.

1 egg
½ cup flour
½ cup oats
¾ cup milk
2 tablespoons honey
1 tablespoon oil
½ teaspoon baking powder
½ teaspoon baking soda
¼ teaspoon salt
¼ teaspoon cinnamon

1. Heat griddle to 300°F, or heat a large frying pan over medium heat.
2. In a mixing bowl, beat the egg well. Add remaining ingredients and mix thoroughly with a whisk.
3. Lightly coat the griddle or frying pan with butter. For each pancake, scoop ¼ cup batter onto the heated surface. When the top of the pancake turns bubbly, flip it and let it cook for another 2 to 3 minutes.
4. Serve with butter and maple syrup.

Makes 12 pancakes.

❧BANANA NUT PANCAKES❧

Serve these delicious pancakes with whipped cream and 100% maple syrup.

2 bananas, mashed
1 egg
1½ cups flour
1 cup buttermilk
1 tablespoon agave nectar
1 tablespoon canola oil
1 teaspoon baking powder
½ teaspoon baking soda
⅓ teaspoon sea salt
½ cup chopped pecans or walnuts

1. Heat a large pan over medium heat, or a griddle to 300°F.
2. In a large mixing bowl, whisk all ingredients together except the nuts. Stir in the nuts last.
3. Lightly butter the hot pan or griddle, then place about ⅓ cup batter per pancake on the hot surface. When the top of the pancakes becomes bubbly, carefully flip them over with a spatula. Cook each side for 3 to 4 minutes.

Makes 8 to 10 pancakes.

Nutrition Tip: Agave nectar is a healthy, all-natural sweetener. According to a study in the *American Journal of Clinical Nutrition*, agave's glycemic index value is about five times lower than that of glucose (table sugar). While Agave nectar has more calories than table sugar, it is sweeter, so you will less of it.

❧HONEY WHEAT PECAN WAFFLES❧

This batter also works well for pancakes.

1 cup whole-wheat flour
1 cup all-purpose flour
2 tablespoons sugar
¾ teaspoon salt
½ teaspoon baking soda
½ teaspoon baking powder
1 egg
1 cup milk
3 tablespoons canola oil
1 teaspoon vanilla
3 tablespoons honey
½ cup finely chopped pecans

1. In a mixing bowl, whisk or sift flour, sugar, salt, baking soda, and baking powder. Make a well in the center of the dry ingredients.
2. In a separate bowl, beat together the egg, milk, oil, and vanilla.
3. Pour the wet ingredients into the well in the dry ingredients, then whisk to combine the wet ingredients with the dry. Add the honey next, combining thoroughly with the other ingredients, then stir in the pecans.
4. Pour ⅓ cup batter onto a hot waffle iron, then close the iron and let waffle cook for 5 for 7 minutes. Enjoy with 100% maple syrup.

Makes 5 to 6 waffles.

PERFECT OATMEAL

*Eating foods with soluble fiber, such as steel-cut oats,
can reduce the risk of heart disease.*

1 cup steel-cut oats
4 cups water
1 cup milk
¼ cup raisins
¼ cup brown sugar
¼ cup chopped pecans
1 dozen strawberries, sliced

1. Boil the oats in the water for 20 to 25 minutes. During the last few minutes of cooking, stir in the milk, raisins, and brown sugar.
2. Scoop into individual bowls. Top each serving with pecans and strawberries.

Makes 4 servings.

CREAM OF QUINOA

This dish tastes similar to breakfast oatmeal or cream of wheat.

1 cup quinoa, uncooked
2 cups water
1 cup milk
2 tablespoons butter
¼ to ½ cup raisins
2 tablespoons 100% maple syrup
2 tablespoons honey
1 to 2 tablespoons brown sugar
1 teaspoon vanilla
1 teaspoon cinnamon (optional)
sliced strawberries (optional)
chopped pecans (optional)

1. Soak the quinoa in a bowl of water for at least 15 minutes, then drain off the water.
2. In a small, covered saucepan, cook the quinoa in 2 cups water. When the water is almost cooked out, stir in the milk, butter, and raisins.
3. Once the raisins have softened, stir in the maple syrup, honey, brown sugar, vanilla, and cinnamon, if using. Remove from heat.
4. If using sliced strawberries and chopped pecans, sprinkle them on top of each serving, to be stirred in by the individual.

Makes 3 to 4 servings.

CARROT NUT RAISIN BREAD

*This bread tastes a lot like carrot cake, but it is healthier
and has just the right amount of sweetness.*

2 carrots
1½ cups whole-wheat flour
¾ cup brown sugar
½ cup canola oil
2 tablespoons honey
1 teaspoon baking powder
½ teaspoon baking soda
1 teaspoon cinnamon
¼ teaspoon salt
1 teaspoon vanilla
3 eggs
½ cup chopped walnuts or pecans
¼ cup raisins

1. Preheat the oven to 325°F. Lightly butter a loaf pan.
2. Purée the carrots in a food processor.
3. In a large mixing bowl, cream together the sugar, oil, and honey. Sift in the flour, baking powder, baking soda, cinnamon, and salt, then stir into the mixture. Add the vanilla and 1 egg at a time and stir well. Fold in the walnuts and raisins. Spread batter in the loaf pan.
4. Bake for 50 minutes. If a toothpick inserted in the center of the loaf does not come out clean, bake the bread for an additional 10 to 15 minutes. Toward the end of baking, if the edges look very dark and the center is not done, drape a piece of foil over the bread to help it finish baking evenly.

Makes 1 loaf.

PASTA DISHES
AND SAUCES

❧MIXED VEGETABLE LO MEIN❧

This is my children's favorite Asian dish. They call it "Chinese noodles."

1 carrot, peeled and sliced
1 celery stalk, sliced
½ red sweet pepper, sliced, stem and seeds removed
1 small zucchini, sliced
10 asparagus stalks, top halves only
½ cup frozen green peas
½ cup chopped red onion
6 ounces (⅓ of an 18-ounce package) spaghetti noodles
¼ cup sesame oil
2 tablespoons soy sauce
2 tablespoons water
1½ tablespoons brown sugar
½ teaspoon salt
⅛ teaspoon pepper

1. Boil the noodles in salt water according to package instructions.
2. Sauté carrot, celery, pepper, and onion in oil for about 5 minutes. Add the rest of the vegetables plus the soy sauce, water, brown sugar, salt, and pepper. Sauté for another 5 minutes.
3. Drain the noodles and add them to the mixture. Cook together for another 5 to 7 minutes, until all the flavors are combined well.

Makes 4 to 5 servings.

Preparation Method: Marinated Raw Asparagus
Set a 12-ounce bag of frozen asparagus on the counter until it defrosts (it will take at least an hour), then drain off the water. In a serving bowl, mix asparagus with 2 tablespoons extra-virgin olive oil, 1 tablespoon balsamic vinegar, ½ teaspoon garlic salt, ½ teaspoon salt, and ¼ teaspoon cracked pepper. Cover bowl and let asparagus marinate for an hour or more, stirring occasionally. Makes 4 servings.

COCONUT CURRY AND VEGETABLES WITH NOODLES

The exotic flavor of curry and the creamy texture of coconut milk come together perfectly in this dish.

1 cup sliced mushrooms

1 cup small broccoli florets

1 cup shredded cabbage

½ bell pepper, sliced

4 green onions, sliced

10 asparagus stalks, cut into 1½ inch segments

2 garlic cloves, minced

3 tablespoons sesame or canola oil

3 tablespoon soy sauce

2 bay leaves

2 teaspoons red curry powder

¼ teaspoon crushed red pepper

1½ cups coconut milk*

1 teaspoon sea salt

¼ teaspoon cracked pepper

½ box spaghetti noodles

1. Boil the noodles in salt water according to package instructions.
2. In a large skillet over medium heat, sauté the vegetables in the oil for about 5 minutes. Stir in the remaining ingredients except for the noodles. Cover and let cook until the mixture is very saucy and creamy and the vegetables are soft but not limp (about 10 minutes).
3. Drain the noodles, then stir them into the vegetable–sauce mixture. Stir until all the noodles are well coated.

*If using canned coconut milk, try Thai Kitchen® or Whole Foods 365™.

Makes 4 servings.

❧THREE-CHEESE BAKED ZITI❧

This aromatic, zesty baked pasta is a winner for any dinner party.

8 ounces (half of a 16-ounce package) ziti pasta

Sauce:
½ cup chopped onion
4 garlic cloves, minced
1½ cups diced tomatoes
3 tablespoons extra-virgin olive oil
¼ cup ground or grated carrot
1½ teaspoons sea salt
1½ teaspoons garlic salt
1 teaspoon dried basil
¼ teaspoon cracked pepper
¼ teaspoon crushed red pepper

Cheeses:
½ cup ricotta cheese
¾ cup grated mozzarella cheese
¾ cup shredded Pecorino Romano cheese

1. Boil the pasta in salt water according to package instructions. Preheat oven to 350°F.
2. In a large saucepan, sauté the onion and garlic in the oil for a few minutes. Add the remaining sauce ingredients. Cook over medium heat for about 20 minutes, stirring occasionally. Using the back of a large spoon, mash the tomatoes a few times during the cooking process.
3. In a mixing bowl, stir together the mozzarella and Pecorino Romano cheese. Reserve ½ cup of this mixture.
4. Drain the cooked pasta and place it in a 9 x 13-inch baking dish. Stir in the prepared sauce, ricotta cheese, and 1 cup of the cheese mixture, making sure everything is combined well. Sprinkle the remaining cheese on top.
5. Bake until all of the cheese is completely melted, about 25 to 30 minutes.

Makes 8 servings.

❧PASTA PRIMAVERA❧

In Italian, primavera means "springtime." In this recipe, the word refers to the fresh vegetables that are combined with noodles and sauce to make a delectable meal.

8 ounces (half of a 16-ounce package) pasta noodles
1½ cups diced tomatoes with juice
½ bell pepper, sliced
¼ medium onion, sliced
1 small zucchini, sliced
15 to 20 asparagus stalks, top halves only
½ carrot, peeled and sliced
3 mushrooms, sliced
2 garlic cloves, minced
3 tablespoons extra-virgin olive oil
2 tablespoons water
1 teaspoon dried basil
½ teaspoon oregano
¼ teaspoon salt
¼ teaspoon cracked pepper
¼ teaspoon garlic salt
½ cup grated mozzarella cheese
½ cup grated Parmesan cheese

1. Boil the noodles in salt water according to package instructions.
2. While noodles cook, sauté the pepper, onion, zucchini, asparagus, carrot, mushrooms, and garlic in the oil, water, and spices.
3. When vegetables are slightly tender, add the diced tomatoes with their juice.
4. Once the flavors have been well integrated (15 to 20 minutes), add the mozzarella cheese. Stir well and let it mix throughout.
5. Drain the noodles, then stir them into the sauce, along with the Parmesan cheese. You may want to sprinkle additional Parmesan cheese on each portion.

Makes 4 to 5 servings.

PESTO

When serving this sauce with pasta, sprinkle diced tomatoes and extra Parmesan cheese over the pasta and pesto.

2 packed cups fresh basil
½ cup pine nuts
2 garlic cloves
¼ cup extra-virgin olive oil
⅓ cup Parmesan cheese
⅓ cup Pecorino Romano cheese

Purée all ingredients in a food processor. Serve the pesto uncooked, stirred into your favorite cooked pasta, tortellini, or ravioli.

Makes 3 cups.

Nutrition Tip: Basil is very high in vitamin K. The herb also inhibits strains of bacteria that have become resistant to commonly used prescription antibiotics. Nutrients found in basil can protect white blood cells, reduce inflammation, and improve cardiovascular health.

❧MEDITERRANEAN PASTA SALAD❧

This meal is perfect on a hot summer day. It is filling but not too heavy.

8 ounces (half of a 16-ounce package) spiral pasta noodles
1 zucchini, sliced
½ bell pepper, diced
½ cup diced red onion
½ cup halved grape tomatoes
½ cup cooked chickpeas
½ cup black olives
2 mushrooms, sliced
¼ cup shredded Parmesan cheese
Pasta Salad Dressing (see below)

1. Boil the noodles in salt water according to package instructions. Add the zucchini and chickpeas to the boiling noodles for the last 2 minutes of cooking.
2. Place the bell pepper, red onion, grape tomatoes, olives, and mushrooms in a large serving bowl. Drain the noodles and add the hot noodles, zucchini slices, and chickpeas to the serving bowl. Then stir in the cheese and the desired amount of dressing.

Makes 5 to 6 servings.

❧PASTA SALAD DRESSING❧

¼ cup extra-virgin olive oil
1 tablespoon balsamic vinegar
½ teaspoon salt
¼ teaspoon pepper
¼ teaspoon dried basil

Stir all ingredients in a bowl with a whisk. Pour desired amount over salad.

Makes about ¼ cup.

SPINACH ALFREDO PASTA

This pasta was born when I ordered fettuccini Alfredo at an Italian restaurant and they gave me the choice of chicken or shrimp as a topping. I asked the server if they had any sautéed spinach to throw on top instead. They did, and the result was fantastic.

8 ounces (half of a 16-ounce package) favorite pasta
½ cup butter
1 cup milk
3 garlic cloves, minced
1 cup Parmesan cheese (plus extra for topping)
2 tablespoons cream cheese
salt and pepper, to taste
Sautéed Spinach (see below)

1. Boil pasta in salt water according to package instructions. While pasta is cooking, make the sauce, then sauté the spinach according to directions below.
2. In a large frying pan over medium heat, melt the butter, then add the minced garlic and cook for 2 minutes. Add milk, cream cheese, Parmesan cheese, salt, and pepper. When cheese is melted and well blended, the sauce is done.
3. Drain the pasta well, then stir into the sauce. Place a scoop of Sautéed Spinach on each serving of pasta, then sprinkle with Parmesan cheese.

Makes 4 servings.

SAUTÉED SPINACH

5 cups fresh baby spinach, packed
¼ cup extra-virgin olive oil
3 garlic cloves minced
salt and pepper, to taste

In a large frying pan over medium heat, cook all ingredients together, stirring frequently, until spinach is just wilted.

FRESH TOMATO SAUCE AND SPAGHETTI

Sauce like this is made almost every day in nearly every kitchen in Italy.

3 or 4 garlic cloves minced
¼ cup chopped onion
3 tablespoons extra-virgin olive oil
1½ cups diced fresh tomatoes*
½ teaspoon dried basil (¼ cup if using fresh chopped basil)
¼ teaspoon garlic salt
¼ teaspoon salt
¼ teaspoon fresh cracked pepper
8 ounces (half of a 16-ounce package) spaghetti noodles
Parmesan cheese

1. Over medium heat, sauté garlic and onion in oil for 2 to 3 minutes. Add tomatoes and spices and cook for 15 to 20 minutes, stirring occasionally.
2. While sauce is cooking, boil spaghetti noodles in salt water according to package instructions. Drain noodles and add to sauce.
3. Sprinkle each portion with Parmesan cheese before serving.

*Frozen or canned diced tomatoes may be substituted.

Makes 3 to 4 servings.

STUFFED MANICOTTI

This is my husband's favorite, and he requests it for every special occasion.

Fresh Tomato Sauce (see page 143)
1 box manicotti noodles
1⅔ cup ricotta cheese
1¼ cup grated mozzarella cheese
1¼ cup grated Parmesan cheese
½ teaspoon salt
¼ teaspoon fresh cracked pepper
2 pinches oregano
2 pinches dried basil

1. Preheat oven to 350°F. Boil manicotti noodles in salt water according to package instructions, then drain.
2. Spread half of the sauce in the bottom of large baking pan.
3. In a mixing bowl, mix together the ricotta cheese, 1 cup mozzarella cheese, 1 cup Parmesan cheese, and spices. Using your fingers, carefully stuff the cheese mixture into the manicotti.
4. Place the stuffed noodles in a single layer in the pan, then cover them with the remaining sauce. Sprinkle the remaining cheese on top. Bake for 20 to 25 minutes.

Makes 5 to 6 servings.

❧ZESTY MARINARA SAUCE☙

Serve this sauce with any pasta, as a pizza sauce, or as a dip for appetizers such as fried mozzarella or fried zucchini. When you are short on time, you may want to use a store-bought marinara sauce; just be sure it does not contain high-fructose corn syrup or harmful preservatives such as BHT and MSG.

4 Roma tomatoes
1 celery stalk
⅓ large white onion
3 garlic cloves
12-ounce can tomato paste
½ cup grated Parmesan cheese
3 tablespoons extra-virgin olive oil
1 tablespoons red wine vinegar
1 teaspoon dried basil
1 teaspoon oregano
½ teaspoon salt
½ teaspoon cracked pepper
½ teaspoon garlic salt

Purée tomatoes, celery, onion, and garlic in a food processor or blender. Place mixture in a large saucepan over medium heat and cook for about 20 minutes, stirring occasionally.

Makes 7 to 8 cups.

Nutrition Tip: In a study done at Princeton University in March 2010, high-fructose corn syrup (also known as corn sugar) was found to be directly linked to obesity, particularly belly fat, and to correlate with blood-pressure malfunctions, heart disease, and cancer. The sweetener has similar effects on the brain as some types of addictive drug abuse (Bocarsly et al, "High-fructose Corn Syrup Causes Characteristic of Obesity in Rats: Increased Body Weight, Body Fat and Triglyceride Levels," *Pharmacology Biochemistry and Behavior*, Nov. 2010, 101–6).

GNOCCHI

Gnocchi freeze very well. Place them in boiling water straight from the freezer, adding just 2 or 3 minutes to the cooking time.

4 medium potatoes
½ cup flour, plus extra for rolling
1 egg
½ teaspoon salt
Zesty Marinara Sauce (see page 145) or Fresh Tomato Sauce (see page 143)
Parmesan cheese for topping

1. Peel the potatoes, then boil them until they are soft all the way through. Remove them from water and let them cool. When the potatoes are cool enough to handle, grate them with a cheese grater into a large mixing bowl.

2. Using your hands, mix the flour and salt into the grated potatoes. Form a well in the center of the mixture, then crack the egg into the well and gently fold it into the mixture.

3. On a lightly floured surface, roll the potato dough into a log shape about an inch in diameter. Cut the dough into small squares (about 1 inch x 1 inch), then press each square gently (only about halfway through) with a fork.

4. Gently drop the gnocchi into boiling salt water and let them cook for 3 to 4 minutes. Remove from water, then top with Zesty Marinara Sauce or Fresh Tomato Sauce and Parmesan cheese.

Makes about 5 servings.

ZESTY PENNE PASTA AL FORNO

In Italian, al forno means "of the oven."

8 ounces (half of a 16-ounce package) penne pasta
28-ounce can crushed tomatoes
3 garlic cloves, minced
1 red bell pepper, sliced
½ onion, sliced
3 tablespoons extra-virgin olive oil
1 teaspoon dried basil
½ teaspoon garlic salt
½ teaspoon salt
¼ teaspoon cracked pepper
½ cup grated mozzarella cheese
½ cup grated Pecorino Romano cheese
½ cup grated Parmesan cheese

1. Boil the pasta in salt water according to package instructions. Drain well. Preheat oven to 400°F.
2. In a bowl, mix the cheeses together. Set aside.
3. In a saucepan, sauté the garlic, onions, and peppers in the oil and seasonings for 5 to 7 minutes. Then pour in the crushed tomatoes and cook for another 8 to 10 minutes. Slowly fold 1 cup of the cheese mixture into the sauce until it is melted and well blended.
4. In a 9 x 13-inch baking dish, mix the pasta with the sauce. Then sprinkle the remaining cheese mixture evenly on top. Bake for 20 to 30 minutes or until all the cheese is melted.

Makes 8 to 10 servings.

❧VEGETABLE LASAGNA☙

*Salad and garlic bread are the perfect accompaniments
to this creamy, nutrient-packed lasagna.*

approximately 15 lasagna noodles
½ cup butter
3 garlic cloves, minced
1 cup milk
2 tablespoons cream cheese
1 cup grated Parmesan cheese
1 teaspoon salt
½ teaspoon pepper

2 cups ricotta cheese
1 small zucchini, sliced and quartered
1 large carrot, sliced
1 cup chopped broccoli
1 cup chopped fresh baby spinach,
  packed
2 tablespoons olive oil
1 cup mozzarella cheese

1. Preheat oven to 400°F. Boil noodles in salt water according to package instructions.

2. In a large pan over medium heat, make the sauce. Melt the butter, then add the garlic and let the mixture cook for 2 minutes. Add the milk, cream cheese, Parmesan cheese, ½ teaspoon salt, and ¼ teaspoon pepper. Stir until all cheeses are melted and blended well.

3. In a mixing bowl, combine all of the vegetables with the oil plus ½ teaspoon salt and ¼ teaspoon pepper.

4. Spread ½ cup sauce in the bottom of a 9 x 13-inch baking dish. Layer the lasagna as follows: 1 layer of noodles (side by side across the dish), 1 cup ricotta cheese, 1 cup vegetables, ½ cup sauce, 1 layer of noodles (in the opposite direction of the bottom layer of noodles—you will need to cut some noodles to make them the right length), 1 cup ricotta cheese, 1 cup vegetables, ½ cup sauce, and 1 layer of noodles (same pattern as noodles on the bottom). Spread the remaining sauce over the last layer of noodles, then sprinkle the mozzarella and Parmesan cheeses on top.

5. Cover lasagna with foil and bake for 35 minutes, then remove the foil and bake for another 10 minutes. Let stand for 10 minutes before serving.

Makes 8 servings.

PORTABELLA MUSHROOM AND EGGPLANT LASAGNA

The mushroom and eggplant taste so succulent in the tomato sauce for this dish.

5 large tomatoes

4 garlic cloves

¼ white onion

4 to 5 large basil leaves (or 1½ teaspoons dried basil)

1½ teaspoons sea salt

1½ teaspoons garlic salt

½ teaspoon cracked pepper

¼ cup extra-virgin olive oil

1 eggplant, diced

1 portabella mushroom, diced

12 to 15 lasagna noodles

2 cups ricotta cheese

2 cups grated mozzarella cheese

1 cup grated Parmesan cheese

½ cup grated Pecorino Romano cheese

1. Boil the noodles in salt water according to package instructions. Drain well.
2. Purée the tomatoes, garlic, onion, and 3 or 4 of the basil leaves (if using dried basil, add 1 teaspoon to the eggplant and mushroom while cooking).
3. In a skillet over medium heat, heat the olive oil and seasonings, then add the mushroom and eggplant and sauté for 5 to 7 minutes. Stir in the puréed tomato mixture and simmer over medium-low heat for 20 minutes.
4. In a mixing bowl, combine the mozzarella, Parmesan, and Pecorino Romano cheeses, plus the last 1 or 2 basil leaves (finely chopped) or ½ teaspoon dried basil.
5. Preheat oven to 350°F. Spread 1 cup sauce in a 9 x 13-inch baking dish. Layer lasagna as follows: 1 layer of noodles (placed side by side lengthwise across the pan), 1 cup ricotta cheese, 1½ cups sauce, 1 cup cheese mixture, 1 layer of noodles (place noodles side by side in the opposite direction of first layer of noodles, cutting the noodles to fit), 1 cup ricotta cheese, 1½ cups sauce, and 1 cup cheese mixture. Add 1 more noodle layer with noodles laid lengthwise, then top with remaining sauce. Sprinkle remaining cheese on top.
6. Place the baking dish on a cookie sheet and bake lasagna for 40 minutes. Let stand 10 minutes before serving.

Makes 8 to 10 servings.

❧FOUR CHEESE LASAGNA❧

I always make this lasagna for Christmas dinner and when special company comes into town. No one even notices there is no meat in it.

1 package lasagna noodles
2 cups ricotta cheese
2 cups grated mozzarella cheese
1 cup grated Parmesan cheese
1 cup grated Pecorino Romano cheese
1½ cups diced tomatoes
28-ounce can crushed tomatoes
½ cup chopped onion

3 garlic cloves, minced
3 tablespoons extra-virgin olive oil
1 teaspoon garlic salt
1 teaspoon salt
1 teaspoon dried basil
½ teaspoon cracked pepper
¼ teaspoon crushed red pepper

1. In a large pot, boil the lasagna noodles in salt water according to package instructions. Drain in a colander.

2. In a large saucepan, heat the oil over medium heat. Sauté the onions and garlic for 1 to 2 minutes. Add the diced tomatoes and cook for 10 minutes. Stir in the crushed tomatoes and seasonings. Cook for another 10 to 15 minutes, stirring occasionally.

3. In a medium mixing bowl, combine the mozzarella, Parmesan, and Pecorino Romano cheeses.

4. Preheat oven to 350°F. Spread 1 cup of sauce in a 9 x 13-inch baking dish. Layer the lasagna as follows: 1 layer of noodles (placed side by side lengthwise over the sauce), 1 cup ricotta cheese (spread evenly over the noodles), 1½ cups cheese mixture, 1 cup sauce, 1 layer of noodles side by side widthwise (cut the noodles as needed), 1½ cups cheese mixture, 1 cup sauce, and 1 layer of noodles (lengthwise). Spread the remaining sauce over the last layer of noodles. Sprinkle with the remaining cheese.

5.   Bake for 35 to 40 minutes. Let stand 5 minutes before serving.

Makes 8 to 10 servings.

❧TORTELLINI SOUP❧

This is the perfect comfort food on a cold day—and the easiest soup you'll ever make.

3 cups vegetable broth
3 cups water
2 cups refrigerated tortellini
2 tablespoons extra-virgin olive oil
½ teaspoon salt
½ teaspoon garlic salt
¼ teaspoon cracked pepper
¼ teaspoon dried basil
¼ cup grated Parmesan cheese

In a stockpot, bring the broth, water, oil, and seasonings to a boil, then add the tortellini. Cook for another 4 to 6 minutes. Sprinkle 1 tablespoon cheese on each serving.

Makes 4 servings.

BAKED MACARONI AND CHEESE

Serve this mouthwatering dish with steamed vegetables,
and you've got yourself a great meal.

1½ cups uncooked macaroni noodles
⅓ cup chopped onion
1½ cups grated cheddar cheese
1 cup milk
2 tablespoons butter
2 tablespoons flour
1 teaspoon salt
1 teaspoon mustard
½ teaspoon pepper

1. Preheat oven to 350°F. Boil noodles in salt water until soft but not overcooked (10 to 12 minutes).
2. While noodles cook, melt the butter in a saucepan, then add flour with a whisk. Continue to stir while adding salt, pepper, milk, and mustard. Mix well and add ½ cup cheese. Stir occasionally until cheese is melted.
3. In a 2-quart baking dish, place onions, ½ cup cheese, drained noodles, and sauce. Stir together, spread evenly in the dish, and top with remaining cheese. Bake for 25 minutes.

Makes 6 servings.

CHEESY VEGETABLE CASSEROLE

This dish pairs healthy vegetables with creamy, cheesy noodles.

1½ cups uncooked noodles
1 can cream of mushroom soup
1 cup milk
½ cup chopped onion
1 tablespoons extra-virgin olive oil
1 carrot, sliced
1 cup frozen green peas
2 garlic cloves, minced
¼ cup chopped red bell pepper
1 small zucchini, sliced
4 to 6 mushrooms, sliced
1 celery stalk, sliced
1 cup chopped broccoli
2 tablespoons butter, melted
½ cup breadcrumbs
½ cup Monterrey Jack or cheddar cheese
1 teaspoon salt
½ teaspoon cracked pepper

1. Preheat oven to 350°F. Boil noodles in salt water according to package instructions. Drain well.
2. In a skillet, sauté the carrots and onions in the oil for 4 to 6 minutes. In a 9 x 13-inch baking dish, mix the cooked noodles with the soup, milk, vegetables, salt, and pepper.
3. Sprinkle the cheese on top of the casserole. Combine the breadcrumbs and melted butter, then sprinkle on top of the cheese.
4. Bake for 40 minutes. Let stand for 10 minutes before serving.

Makes 8 servings.

❧FAUX STROGANOFF❧

*If you don't like mushrooms, substitute the cream of mushroom
soup with cream of asparagus or cream of broccoli soup,
and the mushrooms with 1 cup frozen peas.*

8 ounces (half of a 16-ounce package) egg noodles
¼ cup chopped onion
2 garlic cloves, minced
1 tablespoon extra-virgin olive oil
1 cup Meat Substitute (see page 67)
1 cup sour cream
1 can cream of mushroom soup
1 cup sliced mushrooms
¼ cup milk
2 tablespoons flour
1 tablespoon Bragg® Liquid Aminos*
1 teaspoon salt
½ teaspoon garlic salt
¼ teaspoon cracked pepper
¼ teaspoon paprika

1. Boil the noodles in salt water according to package instructions.
2. In a large skillet, sauté the onion and garlic in the oil for 2 to 4 minutes. Then add the remaining ingredients (except the noodles) and stir until well blended.
3. Drain the noodles and stir them into the mixture in the skillet. For a creamier sauce, add a little more milk.

*Bragg® Liquid Aminos can be found at any health food store or the health food aisle at most grocery stores.

Makes 4 to 5 servings.

SQUASH CASSEROLE

*This is the perfect dinner during autumn harvest time,
when these squash are in season.*

8 ounces (half of a 16-ounce package)
    elbow or butterfly pasta
1½ cups pumpkin or butternut squash,
    cooked and puréed*
1 zucchini, sliced and quartered
1 yellow squash, sliced and quartered
1 cup milk
½ cup butter
⅓ cup chopped onion
¼ cup Parmesan cheese

2 tablespoons cream cheese
1¼ teaspoon salt
1 teaspoon garlic salt
¼ teaspoon pepper

Topping:
½ cup mozzarella or Monterrey Jack
    cheese
2 tablespoons melted butter
½ cup breadcrumbs

1. Boil the pasta in salt water according to package instructions. Drain well. Preheat oven to 350°F.

2. In a large skillet over medium heat, sauté the onions in the butter for 2 minutes. Then add the milk, Parmesan cheese, cream cheese, puréed pumpkin, and seasonings. Cook, stirring constantly, until the cheeses are melted. Gently fold in the zucchini and squash pieces, and continue cooking for 2 to 5 minutes.

3. Place the drained noodles in a 9 x 13-inch baking pan, then stir in the squash–cheese mixture. Sprinkle the mozzarella cheese over the casserole. Mix the breadcrumbs with the butter, then sprinkle over the mozzarella. Bake for 35 to 40 minutes.

*There are two ways to cook pumpkin and butternut squash if you plan to purée it. To bake, cut into large pieces, then remove and discard the seeds. Place the pieces flesh side down on a cookie sheet. Bake at 400°F for about an hour, or until the flesh is very tender and the skin peels off easily. To boil a pumpkin or squash, peel, cut in half, and remove and discard the seeds. Cut the flesh in small pieces. Place in a large stockpot full of water and boil until the flesh is very tender.

Makes 8 servings.

BAKED PASTA AND SAUTÉED MUSHROOMS IN MOZZARELLA SAUCE

Any shape noodle is fine for this dish,
but my favorite is farfalle (bowtie pasta).

8 ounces (half of a 16-ounce) package pasta
Mozzarella Sauce (see page 157)
Sautéed Mushrooms (see below)
½ cup grated Parmesan cheese

1. Preheat oven to 350°F. Boil the pasta in salt water according to package instructions.
2. In an 8 x 8-inch baking dish, combine the pasta, sauce, and mushrooms. Spread evenly, then sprinkle with Parmesan cheese. Bake for 20 minutes.

Makes 4 to 5 servings.

SAUTÉED MUSHROOMS

If serving these delicious mushrooms as a side dish,
be sure to add salt and pepper, to taste.

2 cups sliced white mushrooms
2 to 3 garlic cloves, minced
3 tablespoons extra-virgin olive oil

In a skillet over medium heat, sauté mushrooms and garlic in oil, stirring frequently, until mushrooms are just tender (about 5 to 7 minutes).

Makes 2½ cups.

❧MOZZARELLA SAUCE❧

This rich and creamy sauce can be used on any pasta.

¼ cup butter
2 tablespoons flour
½ teaspoon salt
½ teaspoon garlic salt
¼ teaspoon cracked pepper
1 cup milk
1 cup grated mozzarella cheese

Melt the butter in a skillet over medium heat, then whisk in the flour and seasonings. Whisk in the milk and mozzarella next, stirring until cheese is melted and sauce is smooth.

Makes 2½ cups.

SPINACH AND RICOTTA STUFFED SHELLS

This pasta dish is a fun way to eat spinach, which tastes great with cheese and tomatoes.

1 package jumbo pasta shells
Fresh Tomato Sauce (see page 143)
½ cup ricotta cheese
¼ cup grated mozzarella cheese
3 garlic cloves, minced
1 cup frozen chopped spinach, defrosted, water squeezed out
¼ teaspoon salt
⅛ teaspoon cracked pepper
½ cup shredded Parmesan cheese

1. Preheat oven to 350°F. Boil the shells in salt water according to package instructions. Drain well.

2. In a small mixing bowl, use a fork to mash together the ricotta, mozzarella, garlic, spinach, salt, and pepper. Gently stuff each shell with about 1 tablespoon of the cheese–spinach mixture (there will be extra shells, so use only those that remained intact during the boiling process).

3. Place the stuffed shells in an 8 x 8-inch baking dish. Cover with the Tomato Sauce, then sprinkle with Parmesan cheese. Bake for 20 to 25 minutes.

Makes 3 to 4 servings.

❧MACARONI SALAD❧

This pasta is perfect for a potluck or get-together. Everyone loves it, and it is sustaining enough if there aren't many other meatless options.

8 ounces (half of a 16-ounce package) macaroni noodles
1 cup green peas (defrost if frozen)
¼ cup chopped onion
¼ cup diced bell pepper (any color)
3 tablespoons cream cheese
3 tablespoons canola mayonnaise
½ teaspoon salt
¼ teaspoon crushed red pepper
¼ teaspoon garlic salt
¼ teaspoon cracked pepper

1. Boil the noodles in salt water according to package instructions. Drain well.
2. Place the remaining ingredients in a mixing bowl. Put the hot, drained noodles on top of the ingredients, then stir until the cream cheese and seasonings are mixed throughout.

Makes 8 servings.

YELLOW SQUASH ALFREDO SAUCE

If you want to sneak vegetables into your children's diet, this scrumptious pasta sauce would be a great way to do so. You really can't tell that it contains a healthy vegetable.

½ cup butter
3 or 4 garlic cloves, minced
¾ cup milk
¾ cup puréed yellow squash
1 tablespoon flour
2 tablespoons cream cheese
1 cup shredded Parmesan cheese
salt and pepper, to taste

1. In a skillet, sauté the garlic in the butter for about 2 minutes.
2. Whisk in the milk, puréed squash, and flour. Stir in the remaining ingredients and continue to stir frequently until all of the cheese is completely melted (the sauce shouldn't be lumpy). Season with salt and pepper.
3. Serve with 8 ounces of your favorite cooked pasta.

Makes 3 cups.

SPECIALTY SALADS

❧SUMMER FRUIT SALAD❧

This is a refreshing way to enjoy fresh fruit. I serve it with Three Cheese Quiche (see page 22), Pumpkin Quiche (see page 24), Swiss Mushroom Spinach Oven Omelet (see page 15), or Egg-white Oven Omelet (see page 16).

1½ cups cantaloupe chunks
1½ cups honeydew melon chunks
1½ cups watermelon chunks (optional)
2 bananas, sliced
1½ cups sliced strawberries
1 cup grapes
juice from 1 lime

Combine all ingredients in a bowl at least 20 minutes before serving. For a saucier fruit salad, let it sit longer before serving.

Makes 8 servings.

Nutrition Tip: Watermelon is loaded with vitamin A, vitamin C, and beta-carotene. In addition, this delicious fruit can help reduce the risk of heart disease, asthma, and colon cancer. Watermelon has also been known to alleviate some symptoms of arthritis.

AUTUMN FRUIT SALAD

This seasonal fruit salad is cool and soothing. You'll find that 100% maple syrup makes an excellent, healthy sweetener.

1 apple, cut into chunks
1 cup sliced strawberries
1 cup grapes
¼ cup pomegranate seeds (optional)
¼ cup dried cranberries
¼ cup chopped pecans
2 tablespoons 100% maple syrup
2 tablespoons honey

At least 20 minutes before serving, place all ingredients in a bowl and combine gently.

Makes 4 to 5 servings.

Cooking Method: Sliced Apples

Core 4 crisp apples, then cut each into 8 to 10 wedges. In a large saucepan, combine apples, 1 cup water, 2 tablespoons raw sugar, 2 tablespoons honey, 1 teaspoon cinnamon, and ¼ teaspoon ground cloves. Cook over medium heat, stirring occasionally, for 35 to 45 minutes or until apples are tender. Makes 4 servings.

GREEN AUTUMN SALAD

This mouthwatering combination makes a great meal or side salad.

2 cups salad greens
1 cup fresh baby spinach
½ apple, sliced
¼ cup dried cranberries
¼ cup chopped pecans
1 ounce crumbled feta cheese
Red Grape Vinaigrette (see below)

In a large salad bowl, toss all salad ingredients together, then add desired amount of dressing and toss again.

Makes 6 side salads or 2 main-dish salads.

RED GRAPE VINAIGRETTE

15 to 18 red grapes
⅓ cup extra-virgin olive oil
3 tablespoons red wine vinegar
¼ teaspoon salt
¼ teaspoon cracked pepper

In a blender or food processor, purée the grapes. Whisk all ingredients together in a bowl. Stir well before pouring onto salad.

Makes 1 cup.

❦SPRINGTIME SPINACH SALAD❦

Like best friends, spinach and strawberries balance each other out.

5 cups fresh baby spinach
¾ cup sliced strawberries
Springtime Spinach Salad Dressing (see below)
1 ounce crumbled feta cheese
¼ cup slivered almonds

In a large bowl, toss ingredients together, then add dressing and toss again. Serve immediately.

Makes 8 to 10 side salads or 4 main-dish salads.

❦SPRINGTIME SPINACH SALAD DRESSING❦

½ cup extra-virgin olive oil
2 tablespoons red wine vinegar
½ teaspoon salt or to taste

Whisk together in a small bowl, then toss with salad.

Makes ½ cup.

> Nutrition Tip: In addition to containing antibacterial agents that help fight off infection, cranberries are full of antioxidants that keep arteries healthy. Cranberries can also help protect the brain from neurodegenerative diseases and memory loss caused by aging.

❧SPINACH MUSHROOM SALAD❧

This is a great summertime salad to serve with
just about any pasta or egg dish!

3 cups fresh baby spinach, packed
2 or 3 large white mushrooms, sliced
2 or 3 thin slices of onion, halved and broken apart
1 ounce feta cheese, crumbled
White Wine Vinaigrette (see below)

Toss all ingredients together in a large salad bowl, then gently fold in the desired amount of salad dressing.

Makes 4 to 5 servings.

❧WHITE WINE VINAIGRETTE❧

½ cup extra-virgin olive oil
4 tablespoons white wine vinegar
½ teaspoon salt
¼ teaspoon cracked pepper

In a small mixing bowl, whisk ingredients together.

Makes about ⅔ cup.

MAPLE PECAN SALAD

This salad is a huge crowd pleaser. The different tastes and textures really make your taste buds zing!

4 packed cups dark salad greens
½ cup Maple-spiced Pecans (see below)
3 boiled eggs, chopped
¼ cup dried cherries
¼ cup crumbled feta cheese
Citrus Poppyseed Dressing (see page 168)

In a large bowl, toss together the salad greens, pecans, eggs, dried cherries, and feta cheese. Gently fold in the desired amount of dressing.

Makes 4 servings.

MAPLE-SPICED PECANS

These nuts are perfect atop ice cream, almost any salad, or a standalone snack.

2 cups pecan halves
3 tablespoons 100% maple syrup
¼ teaspoon ground all-spice

1. Preheat oven to 350°F. In a mixing bowl, stir all ingredients together.
2. Spread coated pecans on a cookie sheet. Bake 3 minutes, then stir and bake another 4 to 5 minutes.

Makes 2 cups.

CITRUS POPPYSEED DRESSING

This salad dressing will knock your socks off. Try it once and you'll crave it on salads forever.

¼ cup canola oil
2 tablespoons orange juice
1 tablespoon white vinegar
1 tablespoon apple cider vinegar
1 tablespoon lemon juice
2 teaspoons sugar
½ teaspoon onion powder
½ teaspoon sea salt
¼ teaspoon poppyseeds
⅛ teaspoon ground mustard

In a small bowl, whisk all ingredients together until they are well combined and the sugar is dissolved.

Makes about 1¼ cups.

Nutrition Tip: Apple cider vinegar has been used since ancient times as a health tonic. In modern times, studies have found that it may help prevent diabetes and obesity.

CUCUMBER SALAD

Cucumbers are very cooling, and this is a unique way to serve them.

3 cucumbers, peeled and sliced
1/4 cup extra-virgin olive oil
1/2 cup chopped onion
1 ounce crumbled feta cheese
3 tablespoons balsamic vinegar
1 garlic clove, minced
1 dash garlic salt
salt and pepper, to taste

Combine all ingredients in a bowl.

Makes 6 to 7 servings.

Cooking Method: Ranch Dip
To make your own ranch dip, simply stir 1/2 teaspoon parsley flakes, 1/4 teaspoon sea salt, 1/4 teaspoon garlic powder, and 1/4 teaspoon onion powder into 1/2 cup sour cream. Serve with cut vegetables such as cucumbers, carrots, celery, bell peppers, broccoli, and cauliflower.

CATALINA SALAD

With vegetables, beans, and corn chips, this is a tangy twist on taco salad.

2 cups Meat Substitute (see page 67)
¼ cup water
½ teaspoon salt
⅛ teaspoon cracked pepper
6 cups dark green salad mix
1½ cups kidney beans (if using canned, drain and rinse them)

1 cup grated cheddar cheese
2 Roma tomatoes, diced
½ cucumber, sliced
½ cup diced onions
2 cups Fritos® corn chips
Catalina Salad Dressing (see below)

1. In a small pan over medium heat, cook the Meat Substitute, water, salt, and pepper until the water evaporates (3 to 5 minutes).
2. In another small pan, heat the kidney beans until warm.
3. In a large salad bowl, combine all ingredients. Pour on the desired amount of dressing and gently toss the salad.

Makes 6 to 8 servings.

CATALINA SALAD DRESSING

My incredible husband, Jeremy, was the mastermind behind this salad dressing.

⅓ cup tomato paste
⅓ cup water
2 tablespoons sugar
2 tablespoons white wine vinegar

2 tablespoons onion
1¼ teaspoons honey
½ teaspoons salt

Mix all ingredients together in a blender.

Makes 1 cup.

❧INSALATA CAPRESE❧

*Fresh mozzarella is formed into soft balls and stored in water.
It can usually be found in the grocery store next to the
specialty and foreign cheeses.*

½ pound fresh mozzarella
2 tomatoes
2 tablespoons extra-virgin olive oil
2 teaspoons balsamic vinegar (optional)
1 teaspoon dried basil (or 1½ tablespoons chopped fresh basil)
salt and pepper, to taste

Cut the mozzarella and tomatoes into ½-inch round slices. Arrange on a serving dish, overlapping the slices. Sprinkle the salad with basil, salt, and pepper, then drizzle with oil and vinegar.

Makes 2 to 4 servings.

Cooking fact: Balsamic vinegar originated in the Middle Ages in Italy. It is made from the reduction product of cooked Trebbiano grape juice. As in Italy, dressing just about any salad with balsamic vinegar, extra-virgin olive oil, and salt and pepper gives the dish an aromatic and irresistibly rich flavor. Vinegar contains potassium, magnesium, iron, and calcium.

❧FRENCH SALAD❧

Believe me, it's worth it to spend an extra 5 minutes making your own croutons for this salad.

4 to 5 cups dark green lettuce, packed
4 hard-boiled eggs, chopped
½ pound soft mozzarella cheese, cut in ½-inch pieces
½ apple, cored and chopped
croutons (see below)
3 to 5 tablespoons extra-virgin olive oil
salt, to taste

Tear the lettuce into bite-size pieces. Toss all ingredients together in a large salad bowl. Drizzle desired amount of olive oil on the salad, then add salt and toss.

Makes 4 servings.

❧CROUTONS❧

2 pieces white bread, cut in small squares
3 tablespoons extra-virgin olive oil
1 pinch dried basil
1 pinch oregano flakes

Heat the oil and spices in a frying pan over medium heat. Lightly sweep both sides of each piece of bread in the oil, then cook for about 2 minutes on each side (watch the croutons carefully—they burn easily).

Makes 2 cups.

GREEK SALAD

Greek salad is a complete, delicious meal with
lots of greens, protein, and calcium.

4 cups salad greens, packed
1 ounce feta cheese, crumbled
1 Roma tomato, sliced
2 thin slices of red onion
½ cup whole black olives
¼ cup chickpeas, cooked, drained, and warmed
10 cucumber slices
¼ red bell pepper, sliced
Greek Salad Dressing (see below)

Toss salad ingredients together in a large bowl. Then mix in dressing and serve immediately.

Makes 5 to 6 side salads, or 2 main-dish salads.

GREEK SALAD DRESSING

¼ cup extra-virgin olive oil
2½ tablespoons balsamic vinegar
½ teaspoon oregano flakes
¼ teaspoon salt
¼ teaspoon fresh cracked pepper

Using a wire whisk, thoroughly combine all ingredients in a bowl.

Makes about ⅓ cup.

HONEY MUSTARD CHEF'S SALAD

Chef's salad usually contains diced ham and turkey or chicken. I have substituted these meats with almonds or sunflower seeds, but you won't miss the meat.

2 hard-boiled eggs, diced
1 cup fresh baby spinach
2 cups dark lettuce or salad greens
5 slices cucumber
¼ cup diced tomato
¼ cup diced mozzarella cheese
¼ cup diced cheddar cheese
¼ cup slivered almonds or sunflower seeds
Honey Mustard Dressing (see below)

Toss all ingredients together in a large salad bowl, then gently fold in the desired amount of dressing.

Makes 2 servings.

HONEY MUSTARD DRESSING

This is also an excellent dip for French fries and fried zucchini.

¼ cup mustard
¼ cup honey

In a small bowl, mix ingredients thoroughly with a fork.

Makes ½ cup.

Nutrition Tip: Sunflower seeds are an excellent source of copper, calcium, iron, zinc, and vitamin B$_1$.

CHINESE MANDARIN SALAD

I serve this salad with Spring Rolls (see page 49) and Asian Eggplant Stir-Fry (see page 80), but it makes a great main dish as well.

7 or 8 large, dark green lettuce leaves, torn into bite-size pieces
¼ cup sliced almonds
¼ cup canned mandarin oranges (reserve 1 teaspoon juice for dressing)

4 wonton wraps
1 teaspoon sesame seeds
Mandarin Salad Dressing (see below)

1. Place the torn lettuce in a large salad bowl and sprinkle with sesame seeds, almonds, and oranges.
2. Pour enough oil into a small frying pan to cover the bottom surface. Heat oil over medium heat. Place a wonton wrap in the oil and cook on each side for 2 to 3 minutes, until both sides are crisp and bubbly. Remove from oil and let dry on a paper towel. Repeat the process with the remaining wonton wraps. When they are cool, break them in small pieces and sprinkle them on the salad.
3. Drizzle on the desired amount of dressing.

Makes 4 to 5 side salads, or 1 to 2 main-dish salads.

MANDARIN SALAD DRESSING

¼ cup canola oil
2 tablespoons soy sauce
1 tablespoons honey
1½ teaspoons white wine vinegar
1 teaspoons sugar
1 teaspoon sesame oil

1 teaspoon juice from can of mandarin oranges
1 garlic clove, minced
¼ teaspoon ground ginger
⅛ teaspoon salt

Combine all ingredients in a small mixing bowl, stirring with a wire whisk until the dressing is smooth.

Makes ½ cup.

SPINACH AND PEA SALAD

I love the creamy and flavorful dressing on this green salad.

3 cups fresh baby spinach, packed
1 cup green peas (if frozen, defrost)
½ cup grated carrots
¼ cup slivered almonds
Buttermilk Ranch Dressing (see below)

In a large salad bowl, toss all ingredients together, then gently fold in the desired amount of dressing.

Makes 4 to 6 side salads, or 2 main-dish salads.

BUTTERMILK RANCH DRESSING

1 cup buttermilk
½ teaspoon salt
¼ teaspoon garlic powder
¼ teaspoon onion powder
¼ teaspoon cracked pepper
¼ teaspoon parsley flakes
¼ teaspoon garlic salt

Whisk all ingredients together in a small mixing bowl.

Makes 1 cup.

CAESAR SALAD

This salad is excellent served with garlic bread or as an appetizer to any Italian pasta dish.

1 large head Romaine lettuce, torn into
    bite-size pieces
1 cup croutons (see page 172)

⅓ cup grated Parmesan cheese
Vegetarian Caesar Salad Dressing (see
    below)

Place lettuce, croutons, and Parmesan cheese in a large serving bowl and toss together. Add the desired amount of dressing, then gently toss again.

Makes 4 to 6 side salads, or 2 main-dish salads.

VEGETARIAN CAESAR SALAD DRESSING

Authentic Caesar dressing is made with anchovies. Try this meatless version—you can hardly taste the difference.

1 garlic clove, minced
⅓ cup extra-virgin olive oil
juice from 1 lemon
2 teaspoons Bragg® Liquid Aminos*
½ teaspoon Dijon mustard

¼ teaspoon sea salt
¼ teaspoon cracked pepper

In a small mixing bowl, whisk all ingredients together.

Makes about ⅓ cup.

*Bragg® Liquid Aminos can be found at any health food store or the health food aisle at most grocery stores.

ABOUT THE AUTHOR

Miriam Barton was born in the Gulf Coast region of Texas and was brought up on Tex-Mex, Cajun, and soul food. As a young adult, she lived in Italy, where she learned that life revolves around food, and that the Italian way is to make meals as delicious as possible. Miriam has spent many years learning the art of creative cooking and has mastered vegetarian cuisine as well as a healthy lifestyle. *Meatless Meals for Meat Eaters* is her second cookbook. She also has a healthy desserts cookbook in the works. Miriam, her husband, and their children reside in the Rocky Mountains.

❧ INDEX ❧